Twenty One Days of Fasting & Prayer

THREE POWERFUL WEEKS THAT WILL
TRANSFORM YOUR DESTINY

Prophet Climate Wiseman

Copyright © 2019 by Prophet Climate Wiseman.

All rights reserved. No part of this publication may be reproduced, distributed or transmitted in any form or by any means, including photocopying, recording, or other electronic or mechanical methods, without the prior written permission of the publisher, except in the case of brief quotations embodied in critical reviews and certain other noncommercial uses permitted by copyright law. For permission requests, write to the publisher, addressed "Attention: Permissions Coordinator," at the address below.

Bishop Climate Ministries
93 Camberwell Station Road
London, England SE5 9JJ
www.prophetclimate.net
Email: admin@bishopclimate.org
Tel: +44 7984 115900 (UK)
Tel: +732 444 8943 (USA)

Contents

Preface - "21 Days Revival"..1
Introduction - "The Daniel Fast" 3
Day 1 - "Getting Spiritually Smart" 6
Day 2 - "River Jordan - It's Time To Cross Over"........9
Day 3 - "River Jordan – Element 1"..........................13
Day 4 - "River Jordan – Element 2" 20
Day 5 - "River Jordan – Element 3"..........................25
Day 6 - "River Jordan – Element 4"..........................30
Internal Spirits - "Driving Out The Big 7" 35
Day 7 - "The Canaanites"..37
Day 8 - "The Hittites"..42
Day 9 - "The Hivites – Part 1".................................46
Day 10 - "The Hivites – Part 2"................................52
Day 11 - "The Perizzites – Part 1"...........................58
Day 12 - "The Perizzites – Part 2".............................63
Day 13 - "The Girgashites" 68
Day 14 - "The Amorites"...73
Day 15 - "The Jebusites" 78
External Spirits -
"The Ones You Meet On The Way"............................84
Day 16 - "The Amalekites – Part 1" 85
Day 17 - "The Amalekites – Part 2" 91
Day 18 - "The Edomites" 95
Day 19 - "The Syrians"..100
Day 20 - "The Sidonians"...106
Day 21 - "The Philistines" 111
Testimonies..149
The Seed 118
About The Ministry 155
Other Books By The Author.....................................156

iii

iv

PREFACE

"21 Days Revival"

Howbeit, this kind does not go out except by prayer and fasting (Matt 17:21)

For the past few years, we have always started off the New Year with a time of fasting, prayer, and climbing up the holy mountain to intercede, but this year the Lord spoke to me to hold a special Revival for the first 21 days of the year where we would be fasting, praying, breaking strongholds, and preparing His people to receive God's greatest blessing yet. This book is a result of those daily prayers that led to thousands of lives being changed, transformed, and saved from disaster.

If you want something you have never had before, then you MUST be willing to do what you have never done before! Insanity is doing the same thing over and over but expecting different results. We can so easily get caught up in that cycle without even realizing. Myself personally I had already made plans to do a lot of travelling at the beginning of the year to continue some business developments that have been in the works for the past 2 years. But I made a decision to put God first and give Him the first month of the year. For why should I spend another 12 months going in the same circles, when I can choose to give God the first portion and guarantee that he will bless the remaining 11 months. It's the same principle of the tithe. Give God your first 10% and He'll bless the remaining 90%. And I believe that you should do the same.

You have been wandering around in this hill country long enough; turn to the north. (Deut 2:3)

I believe so strong that the time has come for God to take control of your life and bring you into your promised land. But you have a part to play in order for that to happen. Many people waste their whole lives wandering the mountain just like the children of Israel, thinking that they are waiting on God, but yet God is the one who is waiting on them! It is time for you to rise up and confront those issues which have delayed and stopped your life for too long! It's time for you to come out of those demonic circles! It's time for you to rise up in prayer and take possession of what belongs to you. Your future is waiting, your destiny is waiting, and God is waiting!

Before you begin, you should know that this book can be used anytime of the year; when you feel that you need a fresh beginning or you are about to embark on a new journey, go on this journey of prayer and fasting first and let everything else be smooth sailing.

The prayers you will find throughout this book are meant to be followed on a daily basis. Don't skip ahead to another day, but read only one chapter per day and pray its corresponding prayer points. There are instructions that can only be activated on particular days in your fast.

You will see I have instructed you to pray the prayer points through either 15 or 13 times per day. This only applies to the prayer points for the day. You will pray through the entire list of points, then repeat it the prescribed number of times. *(Please note: It should only take about 30-45 minutes/day to finish these prayer points. They are designed to be declared like confessions. You declare each point once and then move to the next one quickly.)*

INTRODUCTION

"The Daniel Fast"

In the third year of the reign of Jehoiakim king of Judah, Nebuchadnezzar king of Babylon came to Jerusalem and besieged it. And the Lord delivered Jehoiakim king of Judah into his hand, along with some of the articles from the temple of God. These he carried off to the temple of his god in Babylonia[a] and put in the treasure house of his god.Then the king ordered Ashpenaz, chief of his court officials, to bring into the king's service some of the Israelites from the royal family and the nobility— young men without any physical defect, handsome, showing aptitude for every kind of learning, well informed, quick to understand, and qualified to serve in the king's palace. He was to teach them the language and literature of the Babylonians. The king assigned them a daily amount of food and wine from the king's table. They were to be trained for three years, and after that they were to enter the king's service. Among those who were chosen were some from Judah: Daniel, Hananiah, Mishael and Azariah. The chief official gave them new names: to Daniel, the name Belteshazzar; to Hananiah, Shadrach; to Mishael, Meshach; and to Azariah, Abednego. But Daniel resolved not to defile himself with the royal food and wine, and he asked the chief official for permission not to defile himself this way. Now God had caused the official to show favor and compassion to Daniel, but the official told Daniel, "I am afraid of my lord the king, who has assigned your food and drink. Why should he

3

see you looking worse than the other young men your age? The king would then have my head because of you."

Daniel then said to the guard whom the chief official had appointed over Daniel, Hananiah, Mishael and Azariah, "Please test your servants for ten days: Give us nothing but vegetables to eat and water to drink. Then compare our appearance with that of the young men who eat the royal food, and treat your servants in accordance with what you see." So he agreed to this and tested them for ten days. At the end of the ten days they looked healthier and better nourished than any of the young men who ate the royal food. So the guard took away their choice food and the wine they were to drink and gave them vegetables instead.

To these four young men God gave knowledge and understanding of all kinds of literature and learning. And Daniel could understand visions and dreams of all kinds (Dan 1:1-17)

At that time I, Daniel, mourned for three weeks. 3 I ate no choice food; no meat or wine touched my lips; and I used no lotions at all until the three weeks were over. (Dan 10:2-3)

The purpose of this book is to help guide you spiritually and physically as you take part in the Daniel Fast for 21 consecutive days according to the book of Daniel 1:8-16. During the Daniel Fasting, you can eat anytime of the day but you cannot eat any fish, seafood, chicken or meat. Other animal by-products like eggs, cheese, etc. are okay to eat but you must abstain from all flesh. (Keep in mind that if you eat any meat by mistake you must begin all over again from Day 1).

Why is abstaining from meat, flesh and blood, so important during this time? Because your enemies use blood sacrifices to be able to block you. And everything is connected. During these 21 days, you need to be spiritually "clean" so that God can reveal to you every stronghold in your life that you need to bring down. As you read through the daily chapters, you will begin to see some things jump out at you, you will realize certain issues are already at work in your life, and when you pray you will receive the deliverance from it. Other things you will be praying in advance before they have a chance to crop up and ruin your life. And other times you may not know that you face that issue but when you begin to pray you will experience deliverance (coughing, vomit, spitting up blood or mucous, sweating/heat, etc.) This is no cause for alarm, but only a warning to get into serious prayer in that area to totally destroy that stronghold.

Here also are 4 benefits that are going to manifest in your life within the next 21 days:

1. There will be spiritual clearance and cleansing for the coming year
2. Every sickness and diseases must leave your body (Healing for this year)
3. Everywhere you go, I see favor this year.
4. Good health and the anointing, power and energy to accomplish all what you need to accomplish for this year.

DAY ONE

"Getting Spiritually Smart"

"And when the devil had ended all the temptation, he departed from him for a season. And Jesus returned in the power of the Spirit into Galilee: and there went out a fame of him through all the region round about." (Luke 4:13-14)

What would you do if you knew that there were secret codes and special tactics you could employ in order to protect yourself from the devil this year?

Today we are living in a microwave lifestyle, where we want everything now, now, now. We don't want to have to work hard for anything, and forget about waiting. But because of that we often end up living a life of emergency prayer. Where we wait until the problem happens before we start to take action. But this is not the way that Jesus did it. And I believe that we must learn what He did so that we can have the same results. Today we wait until a problem shows up and then we pray; we wait until trouble strikes and then we fast. But it doesn't work that way and was never supposed to. Yes prayer and fasting are so important, but they need to be done in the right way.

If you read your Bible well, how many times do you see Jesus fast? Did he run and pray every time a problem came? Did he call a weeklong fast whenever the Pharisees stirred trouble? No. We only see Him fast once, which was before His ministry started. But what was He doing? I like to call it a pre-emptive attack; He was terminating every terminator before they showed up. He was addressing every problem before it ever happened. He was praying for every provision, every miracle, every blessing He would ever need. And because of that, for the next 3 1/2 years He was able to lockdown the enemy and no evil could touch him. When He had no boat, He walked on the water. When 5000 people were starving, He fed them with only a few fish and loaves of bread. When He needed to pay His tax, fish would vomit up money for him.

The purpose of this 21 Days of Prayer & Fasting is to address every problem now before it arises. We must shut down every trouble before it ever appears in your life. Why wait until the generational curse is activated in your life, why wait until disaster strikes before you act? No, we must act now so that we can have victory for all of this year. Yes through fasting & prayer, you can lock out the devil for a specific period of time, just like Jesus did. The devil will just be going around your fence looking at you but He won't be able to touch you, because you will be bulletproof! Yes during that time nothing from hell can touch you. Because you have already done your part, and no matter what happens a solution will always come!

The following 21 days are meant to be a Sacrifice. That is the whole point. We give it to God first and He will bless us. That means for the next 21 days you will have to give up your time, give up your sleep, give up your money, give up some family time, but after that you will enjoy sweat less victory for the rest of the year!

This book is divided into three sections according to the book of Joshua 3; it is about preparing you to enter your Promise Land. Before God could take the children of Israel up to possess, the first thing they had to do was cross River Jordan. That is why for the first week we will be dealing with River Jordan.

The second week is mainly focused on the Seven Main Territorial Spirits that you need to drive out in order to fully enjoy what God has for you.

And the third week focuses on the external spirits that you meet along the way and that also want what is yours. They are not in the Promise Land but they will try to take you out of it.

Today there are no specific prayer points, I only want you to put your faith into action now and sow your special seed towards this 21 Day Prayer & Fasting Revival. Remember this is all about pre-emptive attack. We are hitting the enemy in every spot. We are dismantling him from every side. I see some of your enemies have already planned to wipe you out this year. They have already visited their shaman, they have already visited their spiritualist, they have been to the witchdoctor, they have prepared their offering, but they don't know that just like Daniel you have dug your knees for divine intervention. Now we must do something before they have chance to manifest in your life! **I SEE VICTORY IN YOUR LIFE THIS YEAR!**

(Please see back of book for instructions regarding seeds)

DAY TWO

"River Jordan - It's Time To Cross Over"

"Now then, choose twelve men from the tribes of Israel, one from each tribe. And as soon as the priests who carry the ark of the Lord—the Lord of all the earth—set foot in the Jordan, its waters flowing downstream will be cut off and stand up in a heap. So when the people broke camp to cross the Jordan, the priests carrying the ark of the covenant went ahead of them. Now the Jordan is at flood stage all during harvest. Yet as soon as the priests who carried the ark reached the Jordan and their feet touched the water's edge, the water from upstream stopped flowing. It piled up in a heap a great distance away, at a town called Adam in the vicinity of Zarethan, while the water flowing down to the Sea of the Arabah (that is, the Dead Sea) was completely cut off. So the people crossed over opposite Jericho." (Josh 3:12-16)

This was God instructing Joshua on how they were to cross over Jordan. Why Jordan? Why did they have to cross River Jordan when they could have just gone around? There are some things that you must confront during this 21 days. For it is this Jordan spirit that has always been flooding your breakthrough, whenever your harvest time has come, Jordan river will come and try to destroy it.

During harvest time, there should be no rain, but River Jordan was flooding. Every time your harvest is around the corner, Jordan begins to flood.

And what is your harvest? It is the result of all your hard work. It is the result of being patient, waiting on God, going without, and then when time for reward comes, Jordan wants to steal it. But this time, we are dealing with Jordan first. This year it shall not cut you off! Every Jordan River of sickness, disease, frustration, fear, bad luck, must die by fire! Yes every spirit of Jordan that has been assigned to wipe away your destiny, your home, your children, your marriage, your finances, your career, we cut it off in the name of Jesus.

I see even people that have been assigned by the devil to bring you down, to drown your destiny, to lie to you, to bring confusion, frustration and shame, but you must shut them out, refuse to listen, don't allow other people to steal your breakthrough. That is the Jordan spirit.

12 Prayer Points To Overcome Every Spirit of Flooding & Hemorrhage

(YOU MUST PRAY 15 TIMES TODAY)

1. Right now I take authority over every spirit of Jordan that has invaded my life in order to bring failure, lack, no results, I bind it, I rebuke it, I command it to die by fire!

2. I take authority over every river Jordan that wants to flood my destiny with failure, die by fire!

3. Every spirit of flooding that waits until my harvest time comes in order to steal my breakthrough at the last moment, I bind you, I rebuke you, I command you to die by fire!

4. I take authority over every spirit of flooding that wants to drown my destiny, die by fire!

5. I take authority over every spirit of flooding that wants to drown my finances, die by fire!

6. I take authority over every spirit of flooding that wants to drown my career, die by fire!

7. I take authority over every spirit of flooding that wants to drown my business, die by fire!

8. I take authority over every spirit of flooding that wants to drown my marriage/relationships, die by fire!

9. I take authority over every spirit of flooding that wants to drown my children, die by fire!

10. I take authority over every spirit of flooding that wants to drown my health, die by fire!

11. I take authority over every spirit of flooding that wants to drown my confidence, die by fire!

12. I take authority over every spirit of flooding that wants to drown my progress this year, die by fire!

DAY THREE

"River Jordan – Element 1"

When the Lord was about to take Elijah up to heaven in a whirlwind, Elijah and Elisha were on their way from Gilgal. Elijah said to Elisha, "Stay here; the Lord has sent me to Bethel." But Elisha said, "As surely as the Lord lives and as you live, I will not leave you." So they went down to Bethel. The company of the prophets at Bethel came out to Elisha and asked, "Do you know that the Lord is going to take your master from you today?" "Yes, I know," Elisha replied, "so be quiet." (2 Kings 2:1-3)

Elisha was one man who was more acquainted with River Jordan then anyone else. In fact he crossed it twice in one day! He did more miracles concerning River Jordan than anyone else, and was the only prophet to match Jesus in terms of miracles. What happened when Jesus got baptized in Jordan? After coming out of the water, the heavens were opened. It was only after Jesus came out of Jordan that he had power.

Yes your willingness to conquer Jordan is the key to every victory in your life! And that is why we are continuing today to deal with Jordan. The spirit of Jordan represents sickness, poverty, discouragement, frustration, generational curse, death, divorce, in short anything that will keep you on the losing side. Anything that crops up to hinder you from moving forward, from receiving all what God has for you.

But what is it that keeps you from crossing that Jordan? What is it that has always hindered you from crossing over? What is it that is keeping you from breaking that circle in your family, that circle of death, that circle of sickness, that circle of poverty? There is one issue we see keep being associated with Jordan. It is the spirit of discouragement. And Elisha knew it very well.

> When the Lord was about to take Elijah up to heaven in a whirlwind, Elijah and Elisha were on their way from Gilgal. Elijah said to Elisha, "Stay here; the Lord has sent me to Bethel." (2 Kings 2:1)

If you read on in the scripture, you see that again and again Elijah keeps telling him to stay behind, and the prophets kept reminding him that his master was leaving him. But what was really happening? God had already chosen Elisha to replace Elijah, Elijah knew it, Elisha knew it, even the prophets knew what was going to happen. But yet it seemed everyone was trying to discourage Elisha from going any further.

I pray that you would become spiritually smart, and that God would give you eyes to see and discern what is going on in the spiritual realm. When you start seeing frustration and discouragement begin to pile up around you, begin to realize something great is coming up ahead.

The devil was using those prophets to try and discourage Elisha, so that he could give up and stop following Elijah. This is a man that had served him diligently, who gave up everything to follow the will of God for his life. And now he was being told that it was all for nothing. Elijah was pressing him to stay behind, the so called prophets were reminding him that he was leaving him today, leaving Elisha to wonder what will happen to him.

But Elisha was smart, he told them to shut up. I believe he said something like this, "Yes I know what the reality is but don't try and discourage me because I've got my eyes on the prize!" The devil was just trying to frustrate him so that he could give up and turn back and stop following Elijah, yet all the while his destiny was there right around the corner waiting for him. The devil was trying to discourage Elisha, to frustrate him so that he could take his eyes off God, and miss all what God has for him. That's why even Elijah said if you see me when I go from you, then you will receive a double portion. But if not, then you won't.

Sometimes when you see so much frustration begin to brew in your life, please know your breakthrough is right around the corner. Be smart, don't let the devil win. Have a strong heart like Elisha. When you see so much hell break loose, people speaking negative things about you, tell them to shut up, be quiet, don't listen, don't entertain those thoughts. When the devil tries to put fear in your heart, resist him with the word of God. Don't just ignore him, open up your mouth and shut him down. It's time to show him who you are, that you're not giving up this time, you need to intimidate the devil.

"Yes I know so be quiet!! Yes I know the reality, yes I see for myself, but don't discourage me! I am standing in faith, I know that God is going to see me through, don't try to take my eyes off that!!!"

Don't take your eyes off your deliverance. Elisha knew he must hold his faith until the very last moment. All what discouragement wants to do is take your eyes off God. If you get them off God, you are not in faith, and then the merciless devil will steal everything from you.

Yes he may be trying to discourage you at home, through your children, in your marriage, through your career, your business, your health. But don't let that discouragement take your eyes off of God and your reward. I believe you have stood long enough, this time you must not back down, you must not give in, you must not quit! You are on the verge of your greatest breakthrough. And you must pass your test!

I know the devil has been trying so hard to separate you from the anointing, but all what you need to do is be like Elisha, don't give up, keep on pursuing. You are going to receive a double portion, double healing, double favor. Discouragement is the biggest stronghold of the enemy; he wants you to lose your focus. May God strengthen your heart so that you can receive all what He has for you.

22 Prayer Points To Cast Out The Spirit of Disappointment

(YOU MUST PRAY 15 TIMES TODAY)

1. Right now I take authority over every spirit of disappointment that I have inherited from my fathers house, from my mothers house, I bind you, I rebuke you, I command you to die by fire!

2. In the name of Jesus, I declare every spirit of disappointment that has been used to hinder and stop my family members, I bind you, I rebuke you, I defeat you, and I command you to die by fire!

3. I take authority over every demon of disappointment that has been assigned over my life, over my destiny, I bind you, I rebuke you, and I uproot you out of my life in Jesus name.

4. Every demon of disappointment assigned over my life as a result of jealousy, I bind you, I rebuke you, I dismantle you, and I command you to die by fire!

5. Right now I take authority over every spirit of disappointment in my body, in my mind, in my finances, in my marriage, in my family, in my career, in my business, I rebuke you, I bind you, I cast you out! Come out!

6. Every spirit of disappointment that has been assigned over my life to cause last minute delays over my documents, my finances, my marriage, today I command it to die by fire!

7. Every spirit of disappointment, every demon of disappointment that has been playing with my life, I bind it in Jesus name.

8. Every spirit of disappointment that has been causing demonic diversions, I bind it. Every road to disappointment I command it to die by fire!

9. Every sprit of disappointment where my marriage is concerned, die by fire!

10. Every demon of disappointment over my finances, I rebuke you in Jesus name!

11. Every demon of disappointment where my career is concerned, where any legal situation is concerned, I command it to die by fire!

12. Every family disappointment, every disappointment over my children and the fruit of my womb, I bind you, I rebuke you, I command you to die by fire!

13. Every demon of disappointment that has been summoned from hell to frustrate my marriage, I command it to die by fire!

14. Every demon that has been attacking those around me, hindering them from helping me, I command it to die by fire!

15. Every evil spirit that has been targeting those who are assigned to help me, making them afraid, causing them to abandon me, I command you to die by fire!

16. Every spirit of witchcraft that has been activated to cause trouble, to cause people not to help me, to cause people to abandon me, I command it to die by fire!

17. I take authority over all those who have been assigned to help me; wherever they are I command them to be released in Jesus name! I command their finances to be

released! I command their health to be released! I command their destiny to be released!

18. Every spirit of disappointment that has been summoned to frustrate me until I give up, I command it to die by fire!

19. Every spirit of disappointment that has been assigned over my mind to always expect disappointment in my life, I cast it out in Jesus name!

20. From today I declare and I decree that everyday in every way my life is becoming better and better!

21. From today I declare and I decree that everyday in every way my destiny is becoming better and better!

22. From today I declare and I decree that everyday in every way my future is becoming better and better!

DAY FOUR

"River Jordan – Element 2"

The company of the prophets said to Elisha, "Look, the place where we meet with you is too small for us. Let us go to the Jordan, where each of us can get a pole; and let us build a place there for us to live. "And he said, "Go." Then one of them said, "Won't you please come with your servants?" "I will," Elisha replied. And he went with them. They went to the Jordan and began to cut down trees.

As one of them was cutting down a tree, the iron axhead fell into the water. "Oh, my lord," he cried out, "it was borrowed!" The man of God asked, "Where did it fall?" When he showed him the place, Elisha cut a stick and threw it there, and made the iron float. "Lift it out," he said. Then the man reached out his hand and took it. (2 Kings 6:1-7 NIV)

What is it that has been sucking you down, trying to drown you, trying to sink your life, your destiny, your children, your career, your health, your marriage, etc.?

I saw a demonic magnetic field that has been activated to attract failure in your life this year, I saw this magnetic demonic field that has been activated to bring down everything that you try to achieve. That's why you must read through this chapter carefully for I have special information and instructions that you must follow to de-activate this demonic magnetic field that has been activated over your life through spiritual powers.

I see every year the same problem keeps repeating itself again and again in order to frustrate you, in order to discourage you, in order to bring you down. Yes one lady had been having so much trouble in her home, having no peace, she just wanted to run away out of the country, she was going mad. I saw in the spirit that somebody had been coming to her house and touching her door, spreading things around. But she didn't believe me. Until her security camera revealed that every Tuesday, a lady from her workplace would come to her house and spread evil around the compound. What was she doing? That woman was activating a demonic magnetic field in order to pull that woman out of her house.

Today every demonic magnetic field that has been activated to attract problems, sickness, failure in your life and your household must be stopped. I prophesy into your life, every demonic magnetic field that have been activated over your life through witchcraft in order to cause failure, sickness, disease, fear, frustration, poverty, lack, I disarm it in the name of Jesus! I render it powerless and helpless over every area of your life!

I want you to understand that this Daniel's Fasting is not just any ordinary fast; these are not just any ordinary prayers. As you fast from anything that has blood, these forces will become helpless and powerless over your life this year. The Lord revealed to me that we must disarm every trouble of the year before it arrives. The days of problems cropping up only after it's too late, those days are over! This year shall be a year of sweat less victory. But we must do our part first. Yes I see that as you continue to keep praying and fasting God is about to avenge you of every trouble you have gone through for the past 7 years! Yes I see every Jordan is about to vomit all what it has drowned in your life!

This is what has been pulling you down every time you try to do something to enhance your life. It is the demonic magnetic force that has been assigned around your life through evil forces. I see this is just like what happened near river Jordan.

Every effort to make progress in your life mysteriously always gets sabotaged. But today as you begin to pray, every demonic magnetic field over your life is going to be destroyed in Jesus name!

12 Prayer Points To Destroy Every Demonic Magnetic Field

(YOU MUST PRAY 15 TIMES TODAY)

1. I take authority over every demonic magnetic field that is assigned to draw away my life; draw away my finances; I rebuke it; I jam it; I jam it, I render it helpless and powerless over my life; I jam it, I jam it in Jesus name.

2. I decree and declare; this year nothing is going to sink my dream, my life, my goals and my vision in the name of Jesus!

3. I take authority over every demonic magnetic field that has been activated through witchcraft; through disobedience; every demonic magnetic field that has been activated in my home drawing away my peace, I rebuke it, I render it helpless and powerless over my life, over my house hold, I jam it; I jam it in the name of Jesus!

4. Every demonic magnetic field that has been activated over my children and my family to sink their income; to sink their success; to sink their destiny, I jam it now; I jam it and I send it back to the sender in the name of Jesus!

5. I take authority, and I jam every demonic magnetic field that has been activated over my life; over my destiny, causing people to reject me; every demonic magnetic field that has been assigned to draw away my favour, to draw away my success I rebuke it, I jam it now, I render it helpless and powerless in my life in the name of Jesus!

6. I take authority and deactivate every demonic magnetic field that has been activated to sink my career, my business, my relationships this year, I rebuke it, I bind it, I jam it, I render it helpless and powerless over my life

and over my household in the Mighty Name of Jesus Christ!

7. Every demonic magnetic field assigned against my life; assigned against my destiny, causing sickness and diseases I rebuke it, I bind it, I jam it; I render it helpless and powerless over my life and over my household in the Mighty Name of Jesus Christ!

8. Every demonic magnetic field assigned against my relationships, against my marriage for this year; causing separation and strife I rebuke it, I bind it, I jam it; I render it helpless and powerless over my life and over my household in the Mighty Name of Jesus Christ!

9. I take authority and jam every demonic magnetic field that has been activated in my working place, in my business place, in my neighbourhood this year, I rebuke it, I bind it, I jam it; I render it helpless and powerless over my life and over my household in the Mighty Name of Jesus Christ!

10. Right now just as the iron did swim for Elisha; I put out my hand and I prophesy to the north, South, East and West; Divine health thou art loosed! Cometh to me now in the name of Jesus!

11. Right Now I prophesy to the North, South, East and West; Money, Wealth thou art loosed! Cometh to me now in abundance this year in the name of Jesus!

12. Right Now I prophesy to the North, South, East and West; Favour, promotion, love, peace, happiness, peace and prosperity thou art loosed! Cometh to me now in abundance this year in the name of Jesus!

DAY FIVE

"River Jordan – Element 3"

Now Naaman was commander of the army of the king of Aram. He was a great man in the sight of his master and highly regarded, because through him the Lord had given victory to Aram. He was a valiant soldier, but he had leprosy. (2 Kings 5:1 NIV)

Have you ever wondered what it is that makes people reject you for no reason? Why everywhere you go you try your best to fit in but somehow someway you always feel as though you never fit? Are you often left feeling empty or unhappy despite having good things in your life?

As we have been dealing with the spirit of Jordan, the Lord revealed to me that it is an evil mark, a spirit of leprosy and outcast that was assigned over your life, which has led you to never be completely happy. No matter how much you try or do there is incompleteness in your life. This is where you get the job or career that you wanted but somehow you are not fulfilled, this is where you get in a relationship but are never satisfied, or you have children but never enjoy them, somehow there is something always following you making sure your life is incomplete, imperfect. Yes I saw a spirit of leprosy manifesting itself as an outcast, causing rejection and lack of happiness in your life. This spirit of leprosy that always manifests itself as an outcast it must die 7 times in the name of Jesus Christ.

But I believe so strong in my spirit that as you have started this journey of fasting and prayer, every form of disgrace and shame that you have been carrying in your body, in your home, in your children, in your relationship, in your finances, in your career, it is uprooted in Jesus name! Yes this year I prophesy and I declare: you will shine like never before. There will be no imperfection in your life! The Lord is taking over and He is going to mysteriously deliver you from every imperfection. Yes whatsoever made you imperfect before, may the Lord mysteriously heal you, may He mysteriously deliver you, may He mysteriously provide for you, may He mysteriously perfect your life. God wants you to enjoy your life AMEN.

> Elisha sent a messenger to say to him, "Go, wash yourself seven times in the Jordan, and your flesh will be restored and you will be cleansed." So he went down and dipped himself in the Jordan seven times, as the man of God had told him, and his flesh was restored and became clean like that of a young boy. (2 Kings 5:10,14 NIV)

The Bible tells us of a Syrian general named Naaman who was healed from leprosy after dipping himself 7 times in River Jordan and his skin became like that of a baby. Nobody knows how it happened, it was not normal, and it did not make sense to the natural mind. But this is just to show you that this year you will receive some divine instructions from God. As you follow them, I see God working supernaturally to give you the desires of your heart. Yes every curse that has been activated over your life in order to make you an outcast, to cause people to reject you, we reject that now in Jesus name. Every demonic mask that was activated over your life in order to hinder you from having a good career, a good marriage, a good life, we command it to die by fire!

As you begin to pray, I see that what brought you down the last 7 years is not going to bring you down again. This time God is exposing the devil and his workshop. You will remain on top! You will stand high and mighty. Yes, this year God is taking over! Just watch and see. This year God is going to focus on you, your star is about to shine!

22 Prayer Points To Destroy the Spirit of Leprosy

(YOU MUST PRAY 15 TIMES TODAY)

1. I take authority over every spirit of leprosy that has been released in my life to make sure I never enjoy my life this year, I command it to Die by Fire Seven Times!

2. I declare every spirit of an outcast that has been assigned over my life to disgrace me and my family I command it to die by Fire Seven Times!

3. I take authority over every spirit of leprosy that has been assigned against my destiny to cause me to be imperfect and destroy my confidence; I command it to die by Fire Seven Times!

4. Right now I pray and confess that this year no fault will be found against my name, my profession, my career or my destiny in the name of Jesus.

5. I rebuke and bind every spirit of self-deception, causing me to carry the false belief that I am 100%; when I am actually leaking. I believe I receive the grace of God to cover every imperfection in my life in Jesus name.

6. Whatsoever hindered me last year from functioning 100%, I rebuke it in the name of Jesus. I command it to die by Fire Seven Times!

7. Anything hindering me from functioning; I believe and confess that whatsoever it is, God is going to drop it out of my life. I command it to die by Fire Seven Times!

8. After Namaan dipped his skin in River Jordan, it was restored to that of a baby's. This year I believe I receive I'll be restored 100%.

9. This year any sprit of hindrance, shame and disgrace over my life must die by Fire!

10. Any leprosy, any spirit of outcast keeping me from getting what I want and what I need in life, I reject it, I bind it, I command it to Die by Fire Seven Times!

11. Any spirit of outcast, any spirit of leprosy, I command it to die by fire Seven Times!

12. I decree and declare; this is the first year where I'm going to shine like never before. I believe I receive: God is going to bring to completion any place where I've not been experiencing happiness.

13. Any place, anybody where I'm not having peace in my life I command it to die by fire Seven Times!

14. I declare the days of me building a house and not living in it; those days are over.

15. Every curse of leprosy from my mother's house, every curse of leprosy from my father's house I rebuke it, I bind it. I remove it, I cast it out I command it to die by fire.

16. I take authority over that spell that was cast on my mother's children, on my father's children. Any curse of leprosy that was released, I believe that from today, every 24 hours I will be happy. I declare every leprosy that was assigned by anyone that is attached to me, every demonic mark put upon my father's house or my mother's house, I break it in the name of Jesus.

17. I declare every spirit that makes me an outcast, I declare this year I will not be rejected again in Jesus name.

18. Every spirit of leprosy from my mother's house; from my father's house that makes me an outcast in my working place, die by fire, I tear it down, I cast it out.

19. In the name of Jesus; right now I take authority over every spirit of leprosy that has been activated over my life, I remove it, I tear it down, I tear it down in the name of Jesus. I cast it out in Jesus name.

20. I believe and confess that I'm no longer an outcast.

21. Every spirit of leprosy that has been assigned over my church; causing people to reject me; misjudge me; I rebuke it, I reject it, I tear it down. I declare the weapons of my warfare are mighty through God!

22. Every spirit of leprosy, every spirit of imperfection I rebuke it; I cast it out, as I anoint my face, I declare this year I command that spirit of outcast to die by fire; die 7 times (repeat x7)

DAY SIX

"River Jordan – Element 4"

And when Jesus was baptized, He went up at once out of the water; and behold, the heavens were opened, and he [John] saw the Spirit of God descending like a dove and alighting on Him. (Matt 3:16)

Then Jesus, full of and controlled by the Holy Spirit, returned from the Jordan and was led in [by] the [Holy] Spirit (Luke 4:1)

Have you been feeling powerless to change or affect your situation? No matter how much you pray, fast, sow your seed, etc. nothing has ever seemed to change? Child of God this is the reason why for the past four days we have been dealing with River Jordan, but I believe through your prayers you have officially crossed over!

If God himself had to take that journey to Jordan, what about you? There are some things in this life you can never have until you get Power. Even Jesus, for 30 years he never did a single miracle, His ministry did not begin until first He had to go through Jordan.

I see before you will try so hard to sort out your situation but no matter what happens it never works out, but it's because you needed Power. Conquering Jordan makes you complete, conquering Jordan gives you the Power to have 100% victory. I see just like Jesus, this Power has come upon you. Now you are ready to go and down tear down the strongholds of the year.

Everything changed after Jesus was baptized in Jordan. From that day, Power came upon Him. I see the Power to get healthy abiding on you. Yes when you have power to become healthy, your body begins to respond positively to every medicine, your body is receptive to healing. I see Power to get wealthy abiding on you; yes from today everything in your life is going to attract favor to you, the right people at the right time at the right places to cause favorable situations to happen to you.

Yes when you are walking in this power, everything about you, the way you talk, the way you think, the way you walk, the way you dress, everything is going to work in harmony together, in perfect synchronization, in order to propel you forward into your destiny.

23 Prayer Points To Receive Power To Destroy The Powers Of The Devil

(YOU MUST PRAY 15 TIMES TODAY)

1. Any potential threat that makes me liable to failure, I reject it in the name Jesus. I command it to die by fire!

2. This year I believe I receive power to destroy every demonic high places erected against my family in the name of Jesus!

3. This year I believe I receive power to destroy every demonic high places erected against my business in the name of Jesus!

4. This year I believe I receive power to destroy every demonic high places erected against my career in the name of Jesus!

5. This year I believe I receive power to destroy every demonic high places erected against my marriage/relationship in the name of Jesus!

6. This year I believe I receive power to destroy every demonic high places erected against my neighborhood in the name of Jesus!

7. This year I believe I receive power to destroy every demonic high places erected against my finances in the name of Jesus!

8. This year I believe I receive power to destroy every demonic high places erected against my house and home in the name of Jesus!

9. This year I believe I receive power to destroy every demonic high places in my destiny in the name of Jesus!

10. This year I believe I receive power to destroy every demonic high places erected in my body through witchcraft in the name of Jesus!

11. I receive power to break down demonic altars. Just like Jesus went about destroying the works of the devil because God was with him, I decree and declare God is with me so I receive power to destroy demonic altars. Every demonic altar I command it to die by fire!

12. This year, I believe I receive power to destroy every demonic altars in my father's house and in my mother's houses in Jesus name!

13. I believe and confess that I shall decree a thing and it shall be established; so I receive power, I receive power to get healed; I receive power to destroy every work of the devil.

14. I believe I receive power to win every court case against me; I receive power to be successful in Jesus name!

15. I believe I receive power to bring down every witchcraft activated against my life. Every witchcraft, I rebuke it, I render it powerless and helpless over my life.

16. I believe I receive power to get wealth; I receive power to operate a successful business in Jesus name.

17. I believe I receive power to get married/have a successful marriage in Jesus name.

18. This year, I believe I receive power to live a good life in Jesus name!

19. This year, I believe I receive power to get wealth in Jesus name!

20. This year, I believe I receive power to be healed in Jesus name!

21. This year, I believe I receive power to be successful in Jesus name!

22. This year, I believe I receive power to be productive and profitable in Jesus name!

23. This year, I believe I receive power to get good cars/good houses/good …. in Jesus name!

INTERNAL TERRITORIAL SPIRITS
(DAYS 7-15)

"Driving Out The Big 7"

"This is how you will know that the living God is among you and that he will certainly drive out before you the Canaanites, Hittites, Hivites, Perizzites, Girgashites, Amorites and Jebusites." (Josh 3:10)

But if you turn away and ally yourselves with the survivors of these nations that remain among you and if you intermarry with them and associate with them, then you may be sure that the Lord your God will no longer drive out these nations before you. Instead, they will become snares and traps for you, whips on your backs and thorns in your eyes, until you perish from this good land, which the Lord your God has given you. (Josh 23:12)

There are seven main territorial spirits that God talks about repeatedly throughout the Old Testament. They were inhabitants of the land that God had promised to the children of Israel. And He promised to drive them out from before them so that they enjoy the good land and good life that God had for them. But God always had his conditions in order to continue enjoying.

> But if you do not drive out the inhabitants of the land, those you allow to remain will become barbs in your eyes and thorns in your sides. They will give you trouble in the land where you will live. And then I will do to you what I plan to do to them.' (Num 33:55-56)

Many people today are living in their Promise Land but not enjoying it to the full because of issues that they refuse to confront. If you allow them, they will be a thorn in your life, though you are in the promise land, you will never FULLY enjoy. But you can be free if you rise up and confront them and deal with them.

> However, when the Israelites grew stronger, they subjected the Canaanites to forced labor but did not drive them out completely. (Josh 17:13)

You can be in the promise land, but still be suffering from fear, still suffering from one or more of these seven spirits. You can't just deny or ignore the problems that you are facing, hoping they will go away. Don't try to contain them, you need to confront them once and for all and drive them out so you can have total freedom!

For the next one-week we will be dealing with all seven of these territorial spirits.

DAY SEVEN

"The Canaanites"

"This is how you will know that the living God is among you and that he will certainly drive out before you the Canaanites, Hittites, Hivites, Perizzites, Girgashites, Amorites and Jebusites." (Josh 3:10)

Today we are beginning to bring down the first Stronghold – Canaanite (this represents the spirit of fear, terror, torment). You ask me why? No matter what you do in life, fear will always be your biggest enemy. When you are in faith, everything can work the way it is supposed to do, but it can be so easy to allow fear to crop in and steal what God has for you. The Lord revealed to me that this year, fear will want to stop you from moving forward, but we are dealing with it now before it ever has a chance to rise up.

Fear is the opposite of Faith. Faith pleases God but fear pleases the devil, and as long as you are in fear you give satan a key to your life. But you must know that fear is a spirit.

Is there anything that you fear? I mean even a spider or a mouse? If you have any type of fear at all, that is to let you know that the spirit of fear rules a portion of your soul, and as long as it remains you can never have complete victory in your life. So I want you to pray so that you can have breakthrough once and for all and discover all that God has for you! This year you must terminate every fear before it crops up to stop your breakthrough. This is the year where you must overcome! You must breakthrough!

During our own 21 Days Revival in London, God revealed to me that there was a spirit of fear living inside one woman's back, behind her spine. She confirmed to me later that it was true that every once in a while she would wake up with a bad pain in that particular spot in her back whenever that spirit of fear was trying to manifest itself in her life. As I began to pray for her, she was grabbing her back saying that she felt so much heat. It was the power of God destroying every nest of fear in her body!

I see the same thing coming upon you as you begin to pray. Every spirit of fear you have inherited from your father's house, from your mother's house, every spirit of fear that has been living in your body, planted into your mind, that always causes you to lose your destiny, that always causes you to have no peace, that wants to make sure you don't enjoy what God has for you, we uproot it now in the mighty name of Jesus!

23 Prayer Points To Overcome Every Spirit of Fear

(YOU MUST PRAY 15 TIMES TODAY)

1. Today every spirit of fear that has been assigned to terminate my life, I rebuke you, I bind you, die by fire! I command you to come out of my body! Come out of my life in Jesus name!

2. Every spirit of fear I have inherited from my father's house, from my mother's house, I bind you, I uproot you, I command you to die by fire! Come out of my body in the name of Jesus!

3. I take authority over every thoughts of fear, every thought patterns that cause me to fear, I uproot them, I wipe them off. I erase every memory from my subconscious that has resulted into fear; I command it to die by fire! Come out of my body; come out of my mind in Jesus name!

4. Every demonic stronghold in my life I command it to die by fire!

5. Every Canaanite spirit assigned to terminate my destiny; my marriage; my children; I rebuke you.

6. In the name of Jesus I terminate every terminating spirit that has been assigned to terminate my life, my career, my health, I bind you I rebuke you, I terminate you, die by fire!

7. I terminate every spirit that has been assigned to terminate my business, my profits, my contracts, my customers, die by fire!

8. Every spirit that has been assigned to terminate my happiness, my joy, my peace, I rebuke you, I bind you I paralyze you, die by fire!

9. Whatsoever has been tormenting me in the morning, tormenting me at night, causing restlessness, I break its powers in Jesus name.

10. Every shadow of darkness in my life, I drive it out in Jesus name.

11. Anything that is being used to create fear in me, to make me lose my relationship with God, die by fire!

12. Every demonic wind that has been sent my way, I rebuke it, die by fire!

13. Every demonic soul ties where my finances are concerned, where my career, business, marriage, destiny is concerned; I break its powers over my life!

14. Anything that is causing trouble, hindering my progress, my finances, my destiny, I rebuke it in Jesus name. I command it to die by fire!

15. Every strange stronghold that is causing fear, causing death in my life, in my finances, I bring it down.

16. Every spirit of intimidation and fear that has been released over my marriage, over my health, over my career, over my finances, I bind it, I rebuke it, I command it to die by fire!

17. Every psychological battle that has been going on in the spirit realm, causing me to defeat myself, I disrupt it in Jesus name.

18. Every self-destructing spirit that has been sent against me in order to make me give up, to quit, to hate myself, I bind it in Jesus name. I command it to die by fire!

19. Any strange spirit that has been monitoring me, I rebuke it in Jesus name.

20. I terminate every terminator before it terminates me. Every spirit of fear, I bring it down, I bring it down, I bring it down in Jesus name.

21. Anything covering my star I rebuke it in Jesus name.

22. May God expose the weakness of my enemies in Jesus name. May He direct me towards their point of vulnerability.

23. I believe I receive the wisdom of God to know how to bring down every spirit of fear in my life in Jesus name.

DAY EIGHT

"The Hittites"

> So Balak son of Zippor, who was king of Moab at that
> time, sent messengers to summon Balaam son of Beor who
> was at Pethor, near the Euphrates River, in his native land.
> Balak said:
>
> "A people has come out of Egypt; they cover the face of the
> land and have settled next to me. Now come and put a
> curse on these people, because they are too powerful for me.
> Perhaps then I will be able to defeat them and drive them out
> of the land. For I know that whoever you bless is blessed, and
> whoever you curse is cursed." (Num 23:5-6)

The Bible tells us about a man named Balak who was so afraid of the Israelites that he wanted to destroy them. So he summoned the most powerful witch doctor at that time, Balaam, to be able to curse them so that Balak could defeat them.

I see that this is exactly what your enemies have done, they are not just thinking bad thoughts towards you, NO! They have gone out of their way to search for a power to be able to curse you so that nothing in your life can move forward, so that they can defeat you, so that they can drive you out, out of your marriage, out of your career, out of a good life! I see every year there is a demonic altar that gets renewed where your life is concerned so that trouble will never end. And the worse thing is when you don't even know that someone is out to get you. You think everything is okay, though you are just hanging in there. But somebody has made up in their mind they are going to destroy you.

42

Please I beg you, this is not the time to be intellectually smart. Don't think that everything is fine, that there are no witches in your life, or that nobody is pursuing the powers of darkness on your behalf! One of our partners was watching from online during our Revival and as I began to talk about Hittites, she thought to herself that she does not have that problem in her life. But anyways, she would still pray because she doesn't know what lies up ahead. But as we began to pray, she began coughing up blood and all sorts of things. She was being delivered there right in her home! I pray God will open your eyes - I see special forces that have been activated from the powers of darkness to be able to defeat you, to make sure you never fulfill your destiny! Yes you! And we must stop them now in Jesus name! We must strike them down! This year no demonic altar is going to be renewed; we are shutting it down in Jesus name!

In that day the Lord with his sore and great and strong sword shall punish leviathan the piercing serpent, even leviathan that crooked serpent; and he shall slay the dragon that is in the sea. (Isaiah 27:1)

Yes this year God is going to slay every witch that have activated failure over your life. Every witch that has caused trouble for you, your children, your health, your marriage, your finances, your career, your destiny, God will strike them down!!!

20 Prayer Points To Destroy Every Spirit of Witchcraft

(YOU MUST PRAY 15 TIMES TODAY)

1. Today every demonic altar that has been activated through witchcraft, I bind it and I command it to die by fire!

2. Every demonic altar that has been raised up to divide my family, I bind it and command it to die by fire!

3. Every demonic altar that has been raised up to make me unproductive and childless, I bind it and command it to die by fire!

4. Every spirit of witchcraft that has been released over my career, I bind it and command it to die by fire!

5. Every spirit of witchcraft that has been assigned to chase me from my job, I bind it and command it to die by fire!

6. Every spirit of witchcraft that has been assigned to bring death in my family, I bind it and command it to die by fire!

7. Every spirit of witchcraft that has been assigned to bring death to my body, I bind it and command it to die by fire!

8. Every spirit of idolism, paganism, and witchcraft, I bind it, I rebuke it, I render it helpless and powerless over my life!

9. Right now I declare that every demonic altar that has my name on it for destruction, I command it to die by fire!

10. Every spell that has been activated to drive out my children, I bind it and command it to die by fire!

11. Every spirit of witchcraft that has been driving away good people from my life, I bind it and command it to die by fire!

12. Every spirit of witchcraft that has been driving away my customers, I bind it and command it to die by fire!

13. Every spirit of witchcraft that has been sending fear of my goods and services to my customers, I bind it and command it to die by fire!

14. Right now, according to Isaiah 27:1, I ask the Lord to slay the head of every Hittite in my life!

15. Right now, according to Isaiah 27:1, I ask the Lord to slay the head of every hired male or female witchdoctor in my life!

16. Right now, according to Isaiah 27:1, I ask the Lord to slay the head of everyone and anyone who has risen against me using witchcraft!

17. By faith, right now I chop off every Balaam in my life and in my destiny in the name of Jesus!

18. By faith, right now I tear down every demonic altars and shrines that have been activated in my life through envy and jealousy!

19. Every demonic consultation against my life, my family, my children, and my destiny, I command them to stop now!

20. Every spirit of Balaam that has been consulted against my success, against my business, against my health, against my ......, I bind it now and I command it to die by fire 7 times!

DAY NINE

"The Hivites – Part 1"

> The men of Israel sampled their provisions but did not inquire of the Lord. Then Joshua made a treaty of peace with them to let them live, and the leaders of the assembly ratified it by oath. But all the leaders answered, "We have given them our oath by the Lord, the God of Israel, and we cannot touch them now. (Joshua 9:14,15,19)

Today we are dealing with the Hivite spirit. The meaning of Hivites is deceit, pretense or naive. People experience Hivite spirits everyday especially in relationships, business, work and mostly our children.

The Bible tells us about the Gibeonites, a people who were a part of the Hivite community. They deliberately planned to deceive the children of Israel of their land. Part of their plan was to deceive Joshua by pretending as if they had travelled from a very far place. They took with them old clothes, shoes etc. Their motive was to preserve their own land while they survived on the provisions of the children of Israel. In addition instead of fighting the children of Israel they tricked Joshua into signing a treaty. Joshua was emotionally influenced and agreed to sign the treaty without enquiring of the Lord.

I saw evil forces that have been assigned to swindle you, but this year we must stop them, we must uproot them. They have kept you in a spiritual loop to make you believe in their lies.

The Hivite/Gibeonite spirit lured Joshua not to consult of the Lord. In our everyday lives, people make decisions without consulting their man or woman of God. The end result or outcome can be devastating and costly. Most signed contracts are full of deception. Many people have lost money as a result of being in deceitful relationships.

Did you ever know that most of the "Get Rich Quick" money schemes are actually scams, operated from the bottom of the sea, by devil agents? Millions of Christians have been robbed of their money and blessing through promised marriage scams, money scams, business scams, relationship scams, winning scams, gold scams. All these are synchronized demonic works that use witchcraft, fear and a strong spirit of deception, taking advantage of your faith, love and kindness. Yes I saw every year someone is always trying to take advantage of your generosity to steal from you spiritually, emotionally, financially and physically.

But this year, I declare you will not be deceived again to leave your position, you will not lose your money, your wealth or health again in the name of Jesus.

That's why you must terminate this spirit. This spirit that uses utility companies, phone companies, friends and especially strangers to swindle your money and resources, we command it to be exposed today! As you pray the following prayer points 15 times today, watch God expose every **Hivites coming on your way. Millions of people have been deceived! You will not fall into such schemes! I prophesy into your life this year, every evil force summoned from hell in order to deceive you must die by fire!** I declare that you will not be deceived, your family will not be deceived, your heart and mind will not be deceived. I declare that whosoever has deceived you emotionally, spiritually, physically or financially, may the Lord God Almighty cause them to vomit everything and let them be exposed.

He hath swallowed down riches, and he shall vomit them up again: God shall cast them out of his belly. (Job 20:15)

This year only the strong will retain riches, only the strong will retain pure love, only the strong will retain health, only the strong will retain good relationships. And that is you!

19 Prayer Points On Destroying Every Spirits of Deception, Delay & Scamming

(YOU MUST PRAY 15 TIMES TODAY)

1. Every powers of darkness that have been activated to deter and deceive me this year, I command them to die by fire!

2. Every spirit of deception that has been assigned to dry me out financially this year, I command it to die fire!

3. Every spirit of deception that has been assigned to dry me out emotionally this year, I command it to die fire!

4. Every spirit of demonic scams that have been designed to deceive me through relationships, through business and false promises, I command them to be exposed and I cut myself off from them today in the name of Jesus!

5. I take authority over every spiritual blackmail from my family; I command it to die by fire!

6. Every financial blackmail from by-ways and strangers in my life I cut it off now and I command them to die by fire!

7. Every demonic soul-ties as a result of strange spiritual relationships in my life, I bind them, I render them helpless and powerless over my life, I command them to die by fire!

8. Right now I tear down every stronghold in my mind and in my emotions that has been built up through

false promises, I tear it down! I tear it down! I tear it down in the name of Jesus Christ!

9. Today I declare that anyone who has been taking advantage of my kindness to abuse my life and my family, I command them to die by fire!

10. Today I declare that anyone who has been taking advantage of my generosity in order to abuse my finances, my properties, my investments and my family, I command them to die by fire!

11. Today I declare that anyone who has been taking advantage of my faith in order to abuse my finances, my properties, my investments and my family I command them to die by fire!

12. Today I declare that anyone who has been taking advantage of my circumstances in order to abuse my finances, my properties, my investments and my family I command them to die by fire!

13. Today I declare that anyone who has been taking advantage of my situations in order to abuse my finances, my properties, my investments and my family I command them to die by fire!

14. Today I command every deceiver that has crossed my path to begin to vomit everything out their life!

15. Today I command every scammer that has crossed my love life to vomit everything in the name of Jesus!

16. Today I command every scammer that has crossed my marriage life to vomit everything in the name of Jesus!

17. Today I command every scammer that has crossed my children's life to vomit everything in the name of Jesus!

18. Today I command every scammer that has crossed my business life to vomit everything in the name of Jesus!

19. Today I command every scammer that has crossed my career life to vomit everything in the name of Jesus!

DAY TEN

"The Hivites – Part 2"

So I have come down to rescue them from the hand of the Egyptians and to bring them up out of that land into a good and spacious land, a land flowing with milk and honey—the home of the Canaanites, Hittites, Amorites, Perizzites, Hivites and Jebusites. (Ex 3:8)

This is how you will know that the living God is among you and that he will certainly drive out before you the Canaanites, Hittites, Hivites, Perizzites, Girgashites, Amorites and Jebusites. (Josh 3:10)

Today we are revisiting yesterday's topic and shedding more light on it. For this is the least spoken issue but the most devastating with long-lasting impact on many believers, grounding them for years, even decades. This is where Joshua failed. But I am determined that you will not fail.

There are things you must cut off and denounce today if you want to make progress this year. This is a crucial decision that you must make, and you must make it now.

This Hiviite spirit of deception is so dangerous that we had to deal with it again. My heart was so burdened with this issue that we had to revisit it a second time. It is one of the major areas hindering Christians today. Nobody pays attention to it, nobody wants to address it, but yet it is one of the issues causing long-term consequences. It is what finished Joshua, but I declare it will not finish you in Jesus name.

Satan is the master deceiver. He deceived Eve in the garden of Eden and our lives changed forever as a result. When the devil wants to detour your destiny, he will bring deception. When he wants to delay you, he will bring deception. When he wants to frustrate you, he will bring deception. To cause you to spend your entire life circling the mountain, never to move on with God.

Yesterday we talked about scams, but it's much more than scams. It's much more than just financial deception. No, anything that has caused you to be involved in something that is not of God, that is deception. You know what I'm talking about, there are things today that are going on in your life that you have no peace about. It could be a relationship, an emotional attachment, a career, a degree, a business, a financial agreement, a legal agreement.

I prophesy into your life: Any commitment you have involved yourself in that has become a burden to you, year after year, this year it is finished in Jesus name. May God give you the power and grace to walk out of every agreement that you have no peace with.

May the Lord lift you up. May the Lord strengthen you supernaturally. May the Lord cause your eyes to open and see things for what they really are. No more deception! This year you will no longer serve anything that does not serve you. This year you will no longer labor for anything that is not productive. This year you will no longer work for anything that is not benefitting your life. This year you will no longer stay in any relationship that does not give you peace. Enough is enough! Every Hivite that wants to waste your time, your energy, your resources, your health, your destiny, DIE BY FIRE!

This spirit works alongside witchcraft, they are all connected, but it is the most sophisticated and cunning of them all. It plays to your weakness, it knows your pressure points, but I pray you rise up in the Lord and shut them down in Jesus name.

We saw yesterday in the book of Joshua 9 that it was the Hivites that brought Joshua down. It was the Hivites that stopped him from the completing the divine mandate God gave to him, to lead the children of Israel to their promise land. Because of the Gibeonites he was always distracted. So long as you are committed to something that is not of God, trouble will never leave your life. It's time now to be free, it's time to cut yourself off.

Please hear what I'm saying. Somebody asked me the other day, why do you keep talking about the devil this, devil that, I believe I'm free I don't need to worry about the devil. The children of Israel never encountered the Canaanites until they began to enter their promise land. They never met the Hittites or the Hivites until they crossed over River Jordan. You may be thinking everything is okay in your life, but if you really want to move on with God, into a land that is large and spacious, into a land flowing with milk and honey, then God says this is what is waiting up ahead. And I have instructed my servant on what to do, just like He did with Joshua, to be able to make sure that we get there. And now we have even done what Joshua has not done. Joshua could not defeat the Hivites, but in the name of Jesus we have conquered them. Yes this week I see a turning point in your life.

I told you a few days ago this is not the time to bring all your intellect and your reasoning. No, just trust in the Lord your God and He will make your paths straight. Your life needs to be straightened out; you are only fooling yourself. God wants to give you more, He wants to get you out of that situation, He wants to get you out of that land of just enough to MORE THAN ENOUGH! But there is what we must do now in order to disarm those strongholds that are waiting up ahead.

54

19 Prayer Points On Destroying Every Spirits of Deception, Delay & Scamming

(YOU MUST PRAY 15 TIMES TODAY)

1. Every powers of darkness that have been activated to deter and deceive me this year, I command them to die by fire!

2. Every spirit of deception that has been assigned to dry me out financially this year, I command it to die fire!

3. Every spirit of deception that has been assigned to dry me out emotionally this year, I command it to die fire!

4. Every spirit of demonic scams that have been designed to deceive me through relationships, through business and false promises, I command them to be exposed and I cut myself off from them today in the name of Jesus!

5. I take authority over every spiritual blackmail from my family, I command it to die by fire!

6. Every financial blackmail from by-ways and strangers in my life I cut it off now and I command them to die by fire!

7. Every demonic soul-ties as a result of strange spiritual relationships in my life, I bind them, I render them helpless and powerless over my life, I command them to die by fire!

8. Right now I tear down every stronghold in my mind and in my emotions that has been built up through false promises, I tear it down! I tear it down! I tear it down in the name of Jesus Christ!

9. Today I declare that anyone who has been taking advantage of my kindness to abuse my life and my family, I command them to die by fire!

10. Today I declare that anyone who has been taking advantage of my generosity in order to abuse my finances, my properties, my investments and my family, I command them to die by fire!

11. Today I declare that anyone who has been taking advantage of my faith in order to abuse my finances, my properties, my investments and my family I command them to die by fire!

12. Today I declare that anyone who has been taking advantage of my circumstances in order to abuse my finances, my properties, my investments and my family I command them to die by fire!

13. Today I declare that anyone who has been taking advantage of my situations in order to abuse my finances, my properties, my investments and my family I command them to die by fire!

14. Today I command every deceiver that has crossed my path to begin to vomit everything out their life!

15. Today I command every scammer that has crossed my love life to vomit everything in the name of Jesus!

16. Today I command every scammer that has crossed my marriage life to vomit everything in the name of Jesus!

17. Today I command every scammer that has crossed my children's life to vomit everything in the name of Jesus!

18. Today I command every scammer that has crossed my business life to vomit everything in the name of Jesus!

19. Today I command every scammer that has crossed my career life to vomit everything in the name of Jesus!

DAY ELEVEN

"The Perizzites – Part 1"

Catch for us the foxes, the little foxes that ruin the vineyards, our vineyards that are in bloom. (Songs Of Songs 2:15)

Today we are beginning to deal with another spirit, another one of the strongholds that the children of Israel had to face. This is the Perizzite spirit. The word Perizzite means no walls. In short, lack of self-control.

Today, many have died, are in jail, have children out of wedlock, have unnecessary health issues, or suffered many other tragedies because of this spirit. It is one of the main reasons why Christians are not enjoying their life today.

God said that if you refuse to confront these strongholds …. **they will become snares and traps for you, whips on your backs and thorns in your eyes (Josh 23:13)**

That's why you must continue to pray daily. These strongholds must come down, you must be determined In order to terminate them.

The job of the Perizzite is to bring shame and disgrace into your life, to cause you to live a life of regret. Many people that are operating under the Perizzite spirit live a secret or double life. They have to hide their addictions and are ashamed to admit who they really are. I'm talking about food addictions, gambling, drug or alcohol abuse, masturbation and other sexual addictions.

When you have no self-control, you can give your money to anyone who asks. When you have no self-control, you don't know when to stop. When you have no self-control, you feel that you are a slave to whatever you give yourself to. But actually you are. The Bible says that **"you become the slave of whatever you choose to obey" (Rom 6:16)**

If you want to conquer this year – this is the one spirit that you need to confront and deal with once and for all. It's time to put your foot down; enough is enough! As long as you allow anything apart from God to master you, you can never have complete victory in this life!

I declare this year - Nothing shall master you, nothing shall steal your joy anymore! Only Jesus is your Master. You shall not be a slave to food! You shall not be a slave to pornography! You shall not be a slave to the TV! You shall not be a slave to alcohol! You shall not be a slave to cigarettes and drugs!

I prophesy into your life, every spirit that wants to bring shame and disgrace into your life through addictions and reckless behaviors, I break its powers, I command it to die by fire! Yes every negative thoughts and strongholds that keep you prisoner to those strange desires, I uproot them now, I command them to be exposed, DIE BY FIRE!

If there is any area I come across while counseling, in which the devil tries to bring disgrace and to cut you off from God's blessing, it is this spirit. It causes you to live a life of shame, you end up hating yourself, you feel powerless, you don't understand why you continue doing what you do even though you want to stop.

But you are not alone. Even Apostle Paul faced this issue:

"I don't really understand myself, for I want to do what is right, but I don't do it. Instead, I do what I hate". (Rom 7:15)

For the last 4 years I saw Perizzite spirits ruining your life, your finances, your health. But this year I see you catching all the little foxes that have been messing up your vineyards.

<u>You need to understand that this is a spirit. It is a stronghold. And it wants to eat your destiny if you continue to allow it.</u> That's why God spoke to the children of Israel, this is one of the strongholds that you MUST bring down! This year you cannot keep going through the same issues. You must rise up now and confront every enemy of your soul! God wants you to enjoy your life and I want you to enjoy your life! And you do not need to be a slave to that addiction any longer! NO, every lack of self-control that has been causing you to life a life of shame and disgrace, to make decisions that you regret, I break it now in Jesus name! I command you to be free! I command your body to be free! I command your mind to be free!

14 Prayer Points On Destroying Every Spirit of Shame & Lack of Self-Control

(YOU MUST PRAY 15 TIMES TODAY)

1. Right now I take authority over every Perizzite spirit that I have inherited from my father's house, from my mother's house, I bind it now, I command it to die by fire!

2. I take authority over every diabolical powers assigned to influence my destiny through friendship, I bind them, I command them to die by fire!

3. I take authority over every diabolical powers assigned to influence my destiny through marriage, I bind them, I command them to die by fire!

4. I take authority over every diabolical powers assigned to influence my destiny through family members, I bind them, I command them to die by fire!

5. I take authority over every diabolical powers assigned to influence my destiny through friendship, I bind them, I command them to die by fire!

6. I take authority over every diabolical powers that have been assigned to influence my decisions through sexual and emotional soul ties, I bind them, I tear them down, I command them to die by fire!

7. I take authority over every diabolical powers that have been assigned to influence my decisions through financial obligations, I bind them, I tear them down, I command them to die by fire!

8. Every spirit of confusion assigned to hijack my career, my marriage/relationship, my job, my children, I command it to die by fire

9. Every spirit of confusion that has been assigned to scatter my customers, my career, my business, I command it to die by fire!

10. Today by the power of the Holy Ghost I command anyone that has been masquerading in my life in order to shame me and disgrace me, I command them to die by fire!

11. Every little foxes that have been trying to break my patience and my life principles in order to scatter my destiny, I command them to die by fire!

12. Every little foxes that have been assigned to break my marriage/my relationship this year, I bind you, I catch you, and I command you to die by fire!

13. Every little foxes that have been assigned in my business, in my career, in order to mess up my plans for this year, I bind you, I catch you and I command you to die by fire!

14. By faith I declare that this year there will be no more bad influence on my way to success. By faith I declare that my life is getting better and better in the name of Jesus Christ!

DAY TWELVE

"The Perizzites – Part 2"

Again the Israelites did evil in the eyes of the Lord, so the Lord delivered them into the hands of the Philistines for forty years.

A certain man of Zorah, named Manoah, from the clan of the Danites, had a wife who was childless, unable to give birth. The angel of the Lord appeared to her and said, "You are barren and childless, but you are going to become pregnant and give birth to a son. Now see to it that you drink no wine or other fermented drink and that you do not eat anything unclean. You will become pregnant and have a son whose head is never to be touched by a razor because the boy is to be a Nazirite, dedicated to God from the womb. He will take the lead in delivering Israel from the hands of the Philistines." (Judges 13:1-5)

I saw this spirit is what has been eating all your potential for the last 7 years, for the last 3 years. After working so hard, you have nothing to show for it as you would have wanted to. But you must rise up and put a stop to it. This year you cannot be a victim to Perizzites anymore!

The Bible talks about a man called Samson, whom God had called to be a judge over the children of Israel. Most people are familiar with this story, but his story is so tragic and pathetic at the same time. He could have been a great man, He could have influenced millions of lives, but instead his wife betrayed him and had his eyes gouged out shortly before his death. Here was a man born with a huge destiny, with great talent and potential from God to be able to lift up the children of Israel and deliver them from the Philistines. Yet he spent his entire life living amongst the enemy and never benefitted anybody but himself. By the time he died, the children of Israel had made no single improvement; they were in the exact same position as they were before he was born. The Bible says that he killed many more Philistines when he died then when he lived. He was a man who died never to see his full potential.

One great man said "The graveyard is the richest place on earth, because it is there that you will find all the hopes and dreams that were never fulfilled, the books that were never written, the songs that were never sung, the inventions that were never shared, the cures that were never discovered, all because someone was too afraid to take that first step, keep with the problem, or determined to carry out their dream."

Millions of people live and die every day without ever fulfilling their potential. Why? Because of Perizzites. When you are called and chosen by God, the devil who sees your potential will assign Perizzites along your way to throw you off course, making sure you never amount to anything. But that is not your portion! No every curse of Samson that wants to hinder you from having a great destiny, from having a great marriage, from having a great life, we command it to die by fire! Whatsoever wants to draw you away from your destiny and keep you from becoming the great man or woman that you are, let it be exposed in Jesus name!

There are some places you need to stop visiting, there are some people you need to stop associating with. Because they are no good for your life. They are Perizzites! Every little foxes that have been destroying your vineyard, that have been destroying your potential, your business, your health, your marriage, your children, your career, your finances, in order to leave you with nothing to show, I command them to die by fire!

I prophesy into your life, may you live to fulfill your potential! May you rise up and become that great man or woman God has called you to be! Yes May God anoint your ears to discern the right advice and not listen to foolishness.

May He anoint your eyes to see the foxes, to see people for who they really are. This year you will not miss your destiny in Jesus name!

Things are getting hotter and we are beginning to ascend just like Joshua did with the children of Israel. That is why you will notice that each day you have been praying the prayer points 15 times each. There is a reason why. The number 15 represents getting better. You must get better in every area of your life. Yes you must increase this year. You must expand! Your marriage must increase! Your home must increase! Your children must increase! Your business must increase

But please make sure you don't miss. You must pray every day; you must pray each prayer point 15 times through! Remember this is the 21 Days Revival - this is the turning point in your life, for this year to be the year like never before, to be the year of sweat less victory, to be the year of supernatural accomplishment. So we are pushing hard, we are taking down our enemies, we are completely destroying them, and we aren't giving them a breathing space. As you continue to pray every day, I see the anointing to overtake your enemies is going to come upon you just like Elijah. Oh yes you are about to surpass every generational curse that has been hindering you!

14 Prayer Points To Uproot Every Spirit of Disgrace

(YOU MUST PRAY 15 TIMES TODAY)

1. I take authority over every powers of darkness that have been assigned in my life to bring confusion this year, I bind you, I command you to die by fire in Jesus mighty name!

2. I take authority over anyone who has been assigned to confuse me and control my destiny, I bind you, I rebuke you, I command you to die by fire!

3. I take authority over my mind, my thoughts, my emotions and my body, I uproot every seed of pride, rebellion and envy, I bind you, I rebuke you, I command you to die by fire!

4. Right now I take authority over every spell that has been assigned to hinder me and have no self control this year, I bind you, I rebuke you, I command you to die by fire!

5. I command every demonic sense of urgency that has been assigned to cause diversion and wastage of time and resources in my life this year to die by fire! I bind you and I rebuke you!

6. Right now I command every demonic council from the land of philistines that are always meeting to plan my down fall for the year, I bind you, I scatter you and I command you to die by fire!

7. Every curse of loneliness and lack of direction in my life that wants to turn my destiny into disgrace, I bind you, I cancel you, I command you to die by fire!

8. Whosoever wants to exploit my weakness in order to destroy my family, my business, my children, my career, my ...., I bind you, I rebuke you, I command you to die by fire!

9. Every spirit of Samson; ever spirit of lack of self-control, I bind it, I rebuke it, and I command it to die by fire in the name of Jesus Christ!

10. I decree and I declare that this year I will have something to show.

11. I decree and I declare that this year I will have progress to show.

12. I decree and I declare that this year I will have profit to show.

13. I decree and I declare that this year I will have wealth and health to show.

14. I believe that this year I receive the anointing to expand my business, to expand my career, to expand my destiny, to expand my .... in the name of Jesus!

DAY THIRTEEN

"The Girgashites"

> When the Lord your God brings you into the land you are entering to possess and drives out before you many nations— the Hittites, Girgashites, Amorites, Canaanites, Perizzites, Hivites and Jebusites, seven nations larger and stronger than you— and when the Lord your God has delivered them over to you and you have defeated them, then you must destroy them totally. Make no treaty with them, and show them no mercy. (Deut 7:1-2)

I want you to know that you are a Strong and Mighty warrior! You are the Blessed of the Lord. Yes I see the Favor of God coming upon you, God is taking control and causing all your thoughts and desires to line up in accordance with His will! I see throughout this fasting and prayer, your spiritual life is going to another level! Your prayer life is going to another level! And because of that you are going to become a terror to the kingdom of darkness, Yes I see you becoming invincible to your enemies in Jesus name!

I pray you have been holding on, I pray you have been standing strong in prayer, I pray you have been enduring through this 21 Days Revival of Prayer & Fasting. For the enemies we are dealing with, they need to be completely destroyed, they need to be completely wiped off, and that takes persistence and total commitment to keep going until you make it!

This week we have been dealing with the 7 different territorial spirits. We started with the Canaanites, then moved to the Hittites; we have taken down the Hivites and also the Perizzites. But there is one characteristic God gave these 7 nations when speaking to the children of Israel, they were larger and stronger than them.

You ask me what am I talking about? Every challenge in life will require a solution, but there are certain challenges that you cannot treat like how you treat everything else. When we talk about these 7 nations, we are dealing with 7 different territorial spirits. These are spirits that govern your family, spirits that have a right to activate themselves in your life. And you will be a fool to think that you can just outwit them by your own intellect. There are certain things where you need divine intervention. You need the hand of God to do it if it will be done.

Whenever you are dealing with one of these 7 territorial spirits, you can't just approach them like you would any other challenge. No you have to completely destroy them, you have to pursue them until they are completely finished.

Today we are dealing with the Girgashite spirit. Girgashite means to enslave or keep in bondage, to hold as captive. A Girgashite is any reoccurring problem in your life, chronic disease (like high blood pressure, diabetes, HIV), negative behavior patterns, children always in and out of jail, etc. Girgashites bring problems that won't kill you directly but force you to live in bondage the rest of your days. They make you vulnerable to other problems.

I declare this year you will no longer be a victim to any Girgashite. Any spirit of bondage and slavery that wants to keep you captive we command it to die by fire! Every inherited disease that wants to keep you captive, we command it to die by fire! Every financial captivity, I command you to come out in the name of Jesus!

But how do you deal with this spirit?

"Inquire, please, of past generations, And consider *and* apply yourself to the things searched out by their fathers. (Job 8:8)

You must begin to do a research into your family history. Check your mother/father, check your grandparents. If they have already died, what did they die from? Are there any repeating patterns or reoccurring issues that your family faces? These are the problem areas that you are at risk of. But if you are wise you can identify them and bring them down.

Remember our scripture for this Revival is all based on Matt 17:21 – *these things can only come out by prayer and fasting.* There are some things that God can deliver you from directly. But there are other things that you must go through, yourself personally you have to take a journey of prayer and fasting in order to break free. <u>And that is why this 21 Days Prayer & Fasting is so critical to your life.</u> Because you need to deal with these issues once and for all. You need to strengthen your prayer life, strengthen your spiritual life, increase the amount of Word that you listen to, increase your giving, strengthen every area, so that no Girgashite will continue to make a reappearance. Yes any problem that keeps showing up every year, every winter, every summer; every demonic problems that show up every 3 months, every 6 months, we command them to die by fire!

I pray you will become spiritually smart and bring down your enemy before they have a chance to destroy you! Terminate the terminator before they terminate you! Yes you can deal with that cancer before it strikes you. You can deal with that high blood pressure, you can deal with that diabetes before it attacks. What brought down your father, what brought down your mother, it doesn't have to bring you down! I take authority over every inherited diseases that are hiding in your body waiting to make an appearance, I command them to come out NOW in the name of Jesus!

Today we are going to pray each prayer point 13 times, for 13 is a spooky number, it is a mysterious number. In short, the way God is going to deal with your enemies is going to be so strange!

12 Prayer Points To Break Every Spirit Of Bondage & Captivity

(YOU MUST PRAY 13 TIMES TODAY)

1. Right now I take authority over every spirit of bondage and slavery that I have inherited from my father's house, and my mother's house, I bind you, I destroy you, I command you to die by fire!

2. Right now in the name of Jesus, I take authority over every generational curse that wants to manifest itself as inherited diseases and sickness over my life, I bind you, I remove you, I command you to die by fire!

3. I take authority over every Girgashite spirit that has been assigned to hold me in bondage this year, I bind you, I rebuke you, I destroy you, I command you to die by fire!

4. Today I declare that any authority: man made authority, spiritual authority or governmental authority, that wants to hold my life, my business, my family, my marriage, my children as captive, I bind you, I rebuke you, I destroy you, I command you to die by fire!

5. Today by the power of the Almighty God I break free from every financial captivity!

6. Today by the power of the Almighty God I break free from every relationship captivity!

7. Today by the power of the Almighty God I break free from every career captivity!

8. Today by the power of the Almighty God I break free from every family captivity!

9. Today I take authority every sickness and diseases, (name the sickness) high blood pressure, cancer, blindness, ... that wants to hold my body and my life as captive, I bind you, I rebuke you, I destroy you, I command you to die by fire!

10. Today I take authority over every inherited sickness or disease that wants to hold my body and my life as captive, I bind you, I rebuke you, I destroy you, I command you to die by fire!

11. Today in the name of Jesus Christ I take authority over every legal situation that wants to hold my life, my career, my business, and my destiny as captive, I bind you, I rebuke you, I destroy you, I command you to die by fire!

12. I break my self free from every powers of darkness. This year, no weapon forged against me shall prosper.

DAY FOURTEEN

"The Amorites"

> And the children of Israel did evil in the sight of the Lord: and the Lord delivered them into the hand of Midian seven years. And the hand of Midian prevailed against Israel: and because of the Midianites the children of Israel made them the dens which are in the mountains, and caves, and strong holds. (Judges 6:1-2)

Oh I see the devil and his army beginning to tremble. Yes I see the strongholds are cracking at the foundation. I see every enemy is about to come tumbling down! Each and every day you have been praying and fasting, I see you growing stronger and stronger. Yes I see your spiritual armor is getting more powerful. Let me tell you, satan fears a man or woman who knows who they are in God and is not afraid to stand up. The devil is in trouble and he knows it! You must continue to press on!

Powerful things are taking place, powerful deliverance is going on as we are driving out the big 7. Today we are dealing with the Amorites – the spirit of pride and humiliation. We saw in Judges 6 the story of how the Amorites oppressed the children of Israel for 7 years, humiliating them, causing them to hide in caves.

The Bible says that the hand of the Midianites prevailed against Israel. But why? Verse 10 tells us:

> And I said unto you, I am the Lord your God; fear not the gods of the Amorites, in whose land ye dwell: but ye have not obeyed my voice. (Judges 6:10)

I see that this is what has been going on in your life for many years. God always wants to lift you up, but the devil has always brought Amorites in order to tear you down. People who are always jealous of you, envious of you, so they try to humiliate you before others to make you run and hide! And because you were afraid of them, you made yourself subject to them and so they have continued their reign in your life.

Amorites are there in the working place; people that want to use their title and position to take advantage of you and to put you down, making things so difficult for you. They are there in the judicial systems, in the social systems. They put this fear inside you which you don't even understand but every time you see them your heart begins to tremble and you lose all your words. You may have done nothing wrong, but they are obsessed with making your life miserable!

But right now I prophesy into your life, anyone that is envious of what God is doing in your life, envious of your career, of your beauty, of your relationships, I command them to die by fire!

The Bible says that the Midianites oppressed the children of Israel for 7 years, but after that God raised up Gideon to deliver them from their hand. **Seven is the number of divine completion, I see the days of your enemies reigning over you has come to an end. Yes this is the year, I see you coming out of every oppression, I see you coming out of every humiliation. I want you to shout 7 Times: "I HAVE NO FEAR!"**

But how do you deal with this Amorite spirit? Some things in life require not only a spiritual action but also a physical. As you have been fasting and praying, you have taken care of the spiritual side of it. But there is something more you must do. You need to confront them. You need to confront that person or that situation which has kept you in fear. Right now I see power coming upon you.

But you must also pray and cast out any form of Amorite that may also be in you. For you can easily have a spirit of pride and not be aware of it. And that pride in you is what can attract other people into your life who are jealous and envious of you, they want to bring you down because they see your gifts, they see your talents, they see how God has made you to shine. But this year, it is coming to an end.

12 Prayer Points To Destroy Every Spirit of Pride & Humiliation

(YOU MUST PRAY 13 TIMES TODAY)

1. Today I take authority over every spirit of humiliation and oppression that I have inherited from my father's house and my mother's house, I bind you, I command you to die by fire!

2. I take authority over every spirit of humiliation and oppression that has been invading my life every year, I bind you, I rebuke you, I command you to die by fire!

3. Every spirit of humiliation and oppression in my family, I bind you, I rebuke you, I command you to die by fire!

4. Every spirit of humiliation and oppression that has been activated in my working place, I bind you, I rebuke you, I command you to die by fire!

5. Every spirit of humiliation and oppression that is at work in my marriage/relationships, I bind you, I rebuke you, I command you to die by fire!

6. Every spirit of humiliation and oppression that has been assigned over my children, I bind you, I rebuke you, I command you to die by fire!

7. Every spirit of humiliation and oppression working against my customers, I bind you, I rebuke you, I command you to die by fire!

8. Every spirit of humiliation and oppression that has been attached to my finances, I bind you, I rebuke you, I command you to die by fire!

9. Every spirit of humiliation and oppression that wants to control my life, I bind you, I rebuke you, I command you to die by fire!

10. Every demonic altars generating humiliation and oppression of spirit, mind, soul and body over my life, I bind you, I rebuke you, I uproot you, I command you to die by fire!

11. Every spirit of humiliation and oppression risen against my progress for this year, I bind you, I rebuke you, I command you to die by fire!

12. I declare and I decree that this year I am getting stronger and stronger, with the help of my God, spiritually, soul, body, financial and family wise!

DAY FIFTEEN

"The Jebusites"

David was thirty years old when he became king, and he reigned forty years. In Hebron he reigned over Judah seven years and six months, and in Jerusalem he reigned over all Israel and Judah thirty-three years.

The king and his men marched to Jerusalem to attack the Jebusites, who lived there. The Jebusites said to David, "You will not get in here; even the blind and the lame can ward you off." They thought, "David cannot get in here." Nevertheless, David captured the fortress of Zion—which is the City of David.

On that day David had said, "Anyone who conquers the Jebusites will have to use the water shaft to reach those 'lame and blind' who are David's enemies." That is why they say, "The 'blind and lame' will not enter the palace."

David then took up residence in the fortress and called it the City of David. He built up the area around it, from the terraces inward. And he became more and more powerful, because the Lord God Almighty was with him. (2 Sam 5:4-10)

I saw in the realm of the spirit, the divine moment for your divine appointment has arrived. But something wants to mess it up. Something spooky has been going around in your life every year and we must stop it. Yes I saw that someone wants to always contaminate your things with diabolic powers in order to cause failure and bad luck in your life. Yes every year someone will always try to poison the people around you by bringing lies against you. They even try to turn you against people who have helped you. This must stop today. This year you are about to rise up to a level you have never been before. There are some things waiting up ahead that you have been dreaming about for a long time; I see God is about to cause them to manifest this year! Yes I see this year God is beginning to install you in your purpose in life! I know you have been in the wilderness for many months, for many years, but God's time has come for Him to take over and accomplish all what He has in His heart for you!

The first thing David did after being appointed as King was march towards Jerusalem to defeat the Jebusites. You must march today. You must eliminate anyone who wants to pollute your destiny for someone has been contaminating your things with the spirit of bad luck.

When God is getting ready to appoint you, there is one final enemy that you must rise up and defeat. It is this one stronghold that stands between you and your destiny. Yes anyone who has been poisoning people around you in order to rise up against you, they must die by fire.

Jerusalem would forever be remembered as the City of David. Even the Bible talks about a New Jerusalem coming down from heaven. But before David conquered it, Jerusalem belonged to the Jebusites, it was a part of their territory.

I see there are some places and some positions that God wants to bring you to this year, these are things that were destined before the foundations of the world, but you must rise up and defeat every Jebusite first. Now is the time you need to identify every Jebusite in your life and bring them down.

But what is a Jebusite? The actual word Jebusite means pollution or to contaminate, poison. And they have one main focus, your mind.

The job of the Jebusite is to pollute your mind in order to put doubt, fear, and frustration towards your destiny. They like boasting all the time, talking about how great they are and how little you are. They love gossip and will tell you lies in order to pollute your mind and start thinking negative thoughts. This is a lying spirit that operates direct from hell to destroy your destiny. They will try to pollute your mind towards your career, your marriage, your health, your church, your destiny. But you must defeat them at any cost.

Jebusites are assigned to target your mind, to target your core beliefs about yourself. You may be fine on your own until you encounter a Jebusite who brings lies to you to try and poison you and make you give up on what God has for you. They want to put hatred in you, suspicion, insecurity, jealousy, and all evil things. And it always happens around the time of your biggest breakthrough. When you are just about to enter your Promise Land, you will meet the Jebusites. Sometimes they can mask themselves as friends, but they always have ulterior motives. Because of their own jealousy and insecurity, they see the potential that is on your life, and they want to bring you down by making you quit on yourself.

But I declare this year you will see your enemies before they see you! You will not quit, you will not give up! Every assignment of the enemy to frustrate you, to put fear in you, to make you give up on what God has for you, I command it to be exposed, I render it powerless and helpless over your life in Jesus name!

Once your mind is poisoned, your judgment becomes impaired. But you need to deal with them. Shut them down. Refuse to listen or believe what they say.

You ask me what am I talking about. Sometimes God will put a desire in your heart and lead you to a specific place, or you are believing Him for a certain breakthrough, like a career, a spouse, a business, etc. You are faithful in everything, but when God is getting ready to bring the fulfillment, the devil always has a heads up, and at that moment He will assign Jebusites to come and throw you off course.

But after praying, I see you victorious, you will not miss your destiny this time, you will not miss your appointment with success. You are blessed forever. Yes every spirit that has been assigned to contaminate your mind, your house with strange smells I command them to die by fire.

Right now I prophesy into your life, every curse of Jebusite that wants to make you forfeit your destiny, I command it to die by fire! Every Jebusite that is waiting to show up when you are on your way to success, every Jebusite that wants to cut you off from your blessing when you are just around the corner, DIE BY FIRE!!

This spirit is no joke! You must get ready! And avoid anyone at any cost that wants to speak negative into your life. You must avoid them like a plague. In 1 Samuel 22 the Bible talks about how 400 men came and joined David in the cave (those who were in distress, those in debt, and those who were discontented). After that is when He began to doubt himself and made a mistake that could have cost him his future. You must always avoid these 3 types of people. Check your friends, check your associations, if they are not building you up, get rid of them NOW!

12 Prayer Points To Destroy Every Spirit of Pollution & Contamination

(YOU MUST PRAY 13 TIMES TODAY)

1. Today I take authority over every spirit of bad habits and pollution that I have inherited from my father's house and my mother's house, I command it to die by fire!

2. I take authority over anyone who has been going around poisoning people against me, in my family, in my work, in my business, in my church, in my neighborhood, I bind them, I rebuke them, I command them to die by fire!

3. Every demonic powers that have been activated in my life in order to pollute & contaminate my career I bind them, I rebuke them, I command them to die by fire!

4. Every demonic powers that have been activated in my life in order to pollute & contaminate my marriage, I bind them, I rebuke them, I command them to die by fire!

5. Every spirit of witchcraft that has been activated to pollute & contaminate my life, I bind you, I rebuke you, I command you to die by fire!

6. Every demonic powers that have been activated in my life in order to pollute & contaminate my children with failure and rejection, I bind them, I rebuke them, I command them to die by fire!

7. Every demonic powers that have been activated in my life in order to pollute & contaminate my business, I bind them, I rebuke them, I command them to die by fire!

8. Every demonic powers that have been activated in my life in order to pollute & contaminate my mind, my house

with strange smells, I bind them, I rebuke them, I command them to die by fire!

9. Every demonic powers that have been activated in my life in order to pollute & contaminate my body with strange smells, I bind them, I rebuke them, I command them to die by fire!

10. Every demonic powers that have been activated in my life in order to pollute & contaminate my life with rejection, I bind them, I rebuke them, I command them to die by fire!

11. I decree and I declare that this year I am strong and I receive a sound mind.

12. I decree and I declare every day and in every way my life is getting better and better in the name of Jesus Christ.

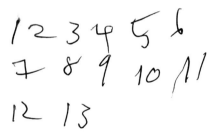

EXTERNAL TERRITORIAL SPIRITS
(DAYS 16-21)

"The Ones You Meet On The Way"

"The Lord replied, "When the Egyptians, the Amorites, the Ammonites, the Philistines, the Sidonians, the Amalekites and the Maonites oppressed you and you cried to me for help, did I not save you from their hands? But you have forsaken me and served other gods, so I will no longer save you. Go and cry out to the gods you have chosen. Let them save you when you are in trouble!" (Judges 10:11-14)

External territorial spirits are not in the Promise Land, but you find them on your way there. Or once you have already possessed and are living in the Promise Land, these are spirits from outside that want to move in and take you out.

These are not like the 7 internal spirits we have already dealt with; for you can still live in the Promise Land while being affected by those spirits. But if you are not careful, these external spirits can utterly destroy you and remove you from your inheritance.

They want to attack you; they want to stop you, from either getting to your promise, or from staying in it. And this is why we need to pray, so that nothing will catch you by surprise this year. Before every external spirit shows up, already they will be disarmed. But it's so important for you to stay covered in prayer, stay spiritually equipped, and always one step ahead of your enemies.

DAY SIXTEEN

"The Amalekites – Part 1"

So Joshua fought the Amalekites as Moses had ordered, and Moses, Aaron and Hur went to the top of the hill. As long as Moses held up his hands, the Israelites were winning, but whenever he lowered his hands, the Amalekites were winning. When Moses' hands grew tired, they took a stone and put it under him and he sat on it. Aaron and Hur held his hands up— one on one side, one on the other—so that his hands remained steady till sunset. So Joshua overcame the Amalekite army with the sword. (Ex 17:10-13)

Child of God, for the whole of last week we have been dealing with the 7 territorial spirits that you must drive out of your Promise Land. These are areas that you need to deal with in order for you to enjoy where God is taking you. For God said,

"But if you do not drive out the inhabitants of the land, those you allow to remain will become barbs in your eyes and thorns in your sides. They will give you trouble in the land where you will live" (Num 33:55).

But there are other external spirits that we have not yet spoke on. These are other dangerous spirits that lie in wait, ready to pounce on you.

The first time the children of Israel encountered the Amalekites was after they had crossed the Red Sea. Imagine they had been in slavery for 430 years, and God had planned for them to rest as soon as they crossed the Red Sea. But they grumbled and complained against Moses and the Lord because they were thirsty. The Bible says, **"they tested the Lord". (Ex 17:7)** As a result, they became vulnerable to their first attack. The Bible tells us that the Amalekites came by surprise, and if not for Moses, it could have been a disaster.

The battle between the Israelites and the Amalekites was not a normal battle. They were not just fighting physically, there was a spiritual battle going on. The Amalekites were devil worshippers. They were devils agents assigned to destroy the children of Israel. And they equipped themselves spiritually before attacking. But my question is, how did the Amalekites see them? Where did they come from? The name Amalek means: a people that licks up; dwellers of the valley.

My God, this type of enemy is so dangerous. They have only one purpose, to destroy you.

But I pray God will remove you from the enemy's radar. Yes anyone that is hunting you to destroy your life, anyone that is laying in wait for you, anyone that is planning a surprise attack, let them die by fire!

You need to know one thing, your enemies are so sophisticated, they are smarter than you. That is why I keep emphasizing that you must throw away your logic and reasoning and just get into prayer. Begin to identify and bring down those strongholds which you know you are vulnerable to.

This year you must equip yourself spiritually. You must strengthen every side. Stop grumbling, stop complaining, stop disobeying God. If there is something you know God is dealing with you about, get over it and let Him work it out. For otherwise you become vulnerable to these attacks. This year – you must avoid grumbling, you must avoid complaining at any cost. If you think God is taking too long to sort out your situation, please don't open up your mouth and sin, just continue to trust in God. It may be that God is just testing your heart.

When you have an Amalekite in your life, you find yourself victim to strange and unexplainable occurrences. Things like bad luck, freak accidents, being struck by lightning, house catching fire, natural disasters targeted towards you, these are the result of Amalekites, of evil wishes.

But I declare right now: Anyone that wants to use supernatural power to bring calamity on your way, I command them to die by fire. Every spirit that has been bringing bad luck and disasters into your life, we drive them out in Jesus name!

There is one thing that the Bible does not mention specifically but if you read between the lines you will see it is there. Moses saw the Amalekites in a vision before they showed up, that is why he was able to prepare Joshua and his army beforehand in order to win. *I see in my spirit, God is going to show you the battle before it takes place. Nothing will catch you by surprise this year in Jesus name! You must be on guard, you must be aware at all times!*

Who were the Amalekites? Amalekites were descendants of Esau, Jacob's brother. They were the relatives of the children of Israel. Amalekites are devils agents. They are filled with hatred, generational hatred. They are godless. Most of the time Amalekites rise up from within your own family in order to destroy you. But I pray God will open your eyes to see them for who they are. The truth of the matter is, Esau and Jacob came from the same womb, but yet God said,

"Jacob I loved, but Esau I hated."(Rom 9:13)

If you find this issue in your family, where there is always a rivalry, jealousy and hatred, etc. begin to mark them and pray. Just because they are your family members, does not mean they will not be used by the devil to try and destroy you.

Amalekites are everywhere. And the chances are that you have already encountered them before. **If you find people hating you for no reason, especially within your family, you need to be delivered from the spirit of Amalekite.** But this year they must not win. As you pray these prayer points, I see the Lord disarming every Amalekite before they reach you!

12 Prayer Points To Destroy Every Spirit of Destruction

(YOU MUST PRAY 15 TIMES TODAY)

1. Today I take authority over every spirit of Amalek, the spirit of disasters and troubles, that I have inherited from my father's house and from my mother's house I forsake you, I bind you and I command you to die by fire.

2. I take authority over every element of surprise that has been activated this year in order to destroy my focus, I bind you, I rebuke you, I command you to die by fire!

3. I take authority over every element of surprise that has been activated this year in order to attack my finances and reverse my progress, I bind you, I rebuke you, I command you to die by fire!

4. I take authority over every element of surprise that has been activated this year in order to destroy my career/my business, I bind you, I rebuke you, I command you to die by fire!

5. I take authority over every element of surprise that has been activated this year in order to destroy my health, my marriage/relationships, I bind you, I rebuke you, I command you to die by fire!

6. As I lift up my voice toward Heaven I ask the Lord God today to rise up and let all my enemies be scattered in the name of Jesus Christ!

7. Today I take authority over every generational hatred that has been bringing down my family, I bind you, I rebuke you, I command you to die by fire!

8. Right now I take authority over every devil agent that has been assigned to monitor me, I rebuke you, I command you to die by fire!

9. Right now I take authority over every messenger of satan that has been assigned to torment me, I command you to fail! I bind you, I rebuke you, I command you to stumble and fall in the name of Jesus Christ!

10. Right now I take authority over every messenger of satan that has been assigned to marry me/work with me/travel with me/partner with me in order to torment and hinder me this year, I bind you, I rebuke you, I command you to stumble and fall in the name of Jesus Christ!

11. Right now I take authority over every messenger of satan that has been assigned to know me/to watch and monitor me/to chat with me/to do business with me in order to torment me and hinder me this year, I bind you, I rebuke you, I command you to stumble and fall in the name of Jesus Christ!

12. By the power of the Holy Spirit I declare and I confess that this year I am moving forward, I am productive and successful in my life in Jesus name!

DAY SEVENTEEN

"The Amalekites – Part 2"

Because the power of Midian was so oppressive, the Israelites prepared shelters for themselves in mountain clefts, caves and strongholds. Whenever the Israelites planted their crops, the Midianites, Amalekites and other eastern peoples invaded the country. They camped on the land and ruined the crops all the way to Gaza and did not spare a living thing for Israel, neither sheep nor cattle nor donkeys. They came up with their livestock and their tents like swarms of locusts. It was impossible to count the men and their camels; they invaded the land to ravage it. Midian so impoverished the Israelites that they cried out to the Lord for help. (Judges 6:2-6)

During this time of fasting and prayer the Lord God revealed to me that every year there are things that are always repeating themselves in your life. I saw a demonic circle over your finances, your family, and your health that has always left you in a very bad shape or position, by the time you recover another comes and leaves you in another bad position. To me it looks there have been a demonic timing, as soon as money comes in things begins to happen and scatter all your money, I see all your efforts and plans in life always being scattered.

Whenever you plan your way, whenever you get money, whenever to try to be happy something will invade and scatter everything, and this always leave you in a bad position. That is the spirit of Amelek, today we must stop it.

I declare this year will be the first complete year in your life where you will plant and you will see and enjoy your harvest, you will plan things and you will see them manifest. Yes I see this year as you join me in prayer especially today every spirit that has been assigned to scatter your career, your finances, your relationship, your health must die by fire. I can feel the anointing right now as I am writing; something is about to happen by the end of the day today. After praying those prayer points 13 times, I see the end to all your unfinished business, yes I see you rewriting your life history.

> What do ye imagine against the Lord ? he will make an utter end: affliction shall not rise up the second time. (Nahum 1:9 KJV)

No it will not happen for a second time. I see you terminating the terminator. This was not a normal battle. But I see you winning.

12 Prayer Points To Bind And Stop Every Scattering Spirit

(YOU MUST PRAY 13 TIMES TODAY)

1. Today I take authority over every demonic circle that I have inherited from my father's and my mother's house that has been causing loss of success and destiny, I rebuke you, I bind you, I command you to die by fire!

2. I take authority over every Amalekite spirit that has been assigned to scatter my career, I rebuke you, I bind you, I command you to die by fire!

3. I take authority over every diabolical powers that have been activated in my life to scatter my family and my relationships, I rebuke you, I bind you, I command you to die by fire!

4. I take authority over every bad dreams that have been used as a channel to manifest problems in my life and in my family, I rebuke you, I bind you, I command you to die by fire! I render you helpless and powerless over my life!

5. Right now I take charge of this year in advance, I close every emotional avenues that have been used to scatter my life and destiny, I rebuke you, I bind you, I close you down, I command you to die by fire!

6. Right now I take charge of this year in advance, I close every spiritual avenues that have been used to scatter my life, my health and my destiny, I rebuke you, I bind you, I close you down, I command you to die by fire!

7. Right now I take charge of this year in advance, I close every financial avenues that have been used to scatter my finances, my savings, my investments and destiny, I

rebuke you, I bind you, I close you down, I command you to die by fire!

8. Right now I take charge of this year in advance, I close every family avenues that have been used to scatter my joy, my peace, my love, my marriage/relationships, my children, I rebuke you, I bind you, I close you down, I command you to die by fire!

9. Right now I take charge of this year in advance, I close every relationship avenues that have been used to scatter and waste my life, my time, my business, my career and my destiny, I rebuke you, I bind you, I close you down, I command you to die by fire!

10. Every genies and territorial spirits that have been planted in my yard, in my home, in my office, outside my house, in my .... today I terminate your purpose in my life and by the power of the Holy Spirit I send you back to the sender in the name of Jesus.

11. Every demonic timing over my life, over my finances, over the works of my hands that have been activated to trigger failure, destructions, and fear, I rebuke you, I bind you, I command you to die by fire!

12. This year I declare and I decree that I will plant and I will reap my own harvest, (name the months left in the year: January, February, March, April, etc. ....) I will plan and I will succeed!

DAY EIGHTEEN

"The Edomites"

But Doeg the Edomite, who was standing with Saul's officials, said, "I saw the son of Jesse come to Ahimelek son of Ahitub at Nob. Ahimelek inquired of the Lord for him; he also gave him provisions and the sword of Goliath the Philistine."

The king then ordered Doeg, "You turn and strike down the priests." So Doeg the Edomite turned and struck them down. That day he killed eighty-five men who wore the linen ephod. He also put to the sword Nob, the town of the priests, with its men and women, its children and infants, and its cattle, donkeys and sheep. (1 Sam 22:9-10,18-19)

I know for years you have been asking yourself questions, why at the last minute things get complicated in your life. But what you did not know is that someone has marked you in the spiritual realm for a sustained attack. I saw too much jealousy and envy against you. And this type of person in your life, year after year they have slowed your progress, undermined your efforts, and frustrated your calling. This has been a heavy baggage for you to carry hence slowing your life down and prolonging your destiny. This can't keep going on and today they must be dealt with. I saw serious information about you that has been used to undermine everything you know and do. This is a new year and if you want it to be different then listen to what I am telling you, you must do things different and the time is now!! Someone or something is seriously scheming on closing all your paths to success this year.

This week we have been dealing with the external spirits you will encounter once you are already in your promise land.

The Edomites are spirits that will come after you are already settled, when God blesses people with a new job, a new home, a new marriage, etc. and then things/people crop up in order to destroy it. This is not your portion. Every person who is so jealous of your promotion, this year they will be cut off.

This year, may God put to an end every person who has been pursuing you for the past 3 years, for the past 7 years. Whosoever has been pretending to be a friend yet has been planning your downfall, let them die by fire! I prophesy and declare: if they will not stand with you they will not stand at all!

The Bible tells us that David fled from Saul to Nob and went to the Ahimelek the priest. Starving for food, he asked the priest for bread and a sword, who not knowing that he was on the run, gave him provisions as he had always done in the past. But Doeg, the Edomite, was there that day and told Saul the enemy of David all what had happened. Then he the Edomite utterly destroyed Ahimelek and all his family when Sauls own army refused to raise their hand against him.

An Edomite is that person who is waiting for the opportunity to strike you down. You find them in your working place, in your family, in your church. They go behind your back; they try to get key information about your life, pretending to be less concerned yet they are on your case, always being driven by serious ulterior motives. They pretend to be minding their business, yet they are only after your position. They pretend to want to help; yet they are after your relationship. An Edomite will sell you out to the authorities even though you have helped them before. They are wicked to the heart and nothing you do can help them.

I saw a messenger of satan appointed to torment and frustrate you. They must come down, and today they will. David was so frustrated by this particular person that he prayed this dangerous prayer and God answered him by sending three Angels. God sent three "Angels of destruction" to Doeg; the first caused him to forget his learning, the second burned his soul, and the third scattered the ashes.

Why do you boast of evil, you mighty hero? Why do you boast all day long, you who are a disgrace in the eyes of God?

You who practice deceit, your tongue plots destruction; it is like a sharpened razor. You love evil rather than good, falsehood rather than speaking the truth. You love every harmful word, you deceitful tongue!

Surely God will bring you down to everlasting ruin: He will snatch you up and pluck you from your tent; he will uproot you from the land of the living. (Ps 52:1-5)

I believe that if God answered David He will answer you today, I saw the same ancient angels ready to be dispatched to minister justice on your behalf. Whosoever has been undermining your efforts must die by fire. You must pray now. I have serious Powerful prayer points, your Doeg will not survive in this year; every document or information held against you must disappear. That's why you must pray **13 TIMES!!!!!!**

This is what God is going to do to your enemies! This year no Edomite will raise up their voice a second time. Every harmful words that they have been spreading in order to taint your reputation, we command them to die by fire! Every evil tongue, every evil eye that is after your life, your relationships, your career, your children, your destiny, right now we destroy it in Jesus name!

12 Prayer Points To Destroy Every Spirit of Malice & Envy

(YOU MUST PRAY 13 TIMES TODAY)

1. Today in the name of Jesus I take authority over every curse of Edomite that has been causing envy and jealousy in my father's and my mother's house, I uproot you, I bind you, I rebuke you, I command you to die by fire!

2. Today I take authority over anyone and anything that has been boasting against my life and my achievements for this year. May the Lord God turn them to disgrace.

3. I pray and I declare that this year the Lord God will disgrace every enemy of progress in my life in the name of Jesus Christ.

4. I pray and I declare that this year the Lord God will disgrace every enemy of my business in the name of Jesus Christ.

5. I pray and I declare that this year the Lord God will disgrace every Edomite spirit of envy and jealousy in my life in the name of Jesus Christ.

6. I pray and I declare that this year the Lord God will disgrace by daytime every enemy of my success and career in the name of Jesus Christ.

7. I pray and I declare that this year the Lord God will disgrace every enemy of my household and investments in the name of Jesus Christ.

8. Today I take authority over every tongue of destruction that have risen up against me, against my purpose, I bind it, I rebuke it, I command it to die by fire!

9. Right now I take authority over anyone who has been going around speaking falsehood and malice against me to set me up for failure and disgrace, I bind them, I rebuke them, I render them helpless and powerless over my life in the name of Jesus Christ!

10. Right now I take authority over every harmful word written or spoken that has been assigned to destroy my career, my relationships/marriage, my .... I bind it, I uproot it, I destroy it, I render it helpless and powerless over my life in the name of Jesus Christ!

11. I command every Edomite person or situation in my life to be exposed. This year I declare and I decree that the lord will snatch them, tear them up and uproot them from the land of the living.

12. I declare and I decree that this year, my life will be stable, spiritually, soul, body, financially and socially in the name of Jesus Christ.

Now angels thou are loosed! Go forth and bring a physical manifestation of these prayers and words that I have spoken in Jesus mighty name.

DAY NINETEEN

"The Syrians"

Now the king of Aram was at war with Israel. After conferring with his officers, he said, "I will set up my camp in such and such a place." The man of God sent word to the king of Israel: "Beware of passing that place, because the Arameans are going down there." So the king of Israel checked on the place indicated by the man of God. Time and again Elisha warned the king, so that he was on his guard in such places. This enraged the king of Aram. He summoned his officers and demanded of them, "Tell me! Which of us is on the side of the king of Israel?"

"None of us, my lord the king," said one of his officers, "but Elisha, the prophet who is in Israel, tells the king of Israel the very words you speak in your bedroom."

"Go, find out where he is," the king ordered, "so I can send men and capture him." The report came back: "He is in Dothan." Then he sent horses and chariots and a strong force there. They went by night and surrounded the city. (2 Kings 6:8-14)

This year God is about to raise you up, He is about to take you to another level, there is a promotion that is coming on the way, that breakthrough which you have been waiting on for so long, it is just around the corner! But you must get into serious prayers. I believe every day you have been praying, you have been fasting, and now we are almost there, only 2 more days to go, but every demon is on high alert. Yes though we have disarmed every Canaanite, we have disarmed every Hittite, we have driven out every internal spirit, but there are some other spirits that come with the territory, they must be expected, and they must be dealt with.

You ask me what am I talking about? Every new level comes with a new devil. Yes, every new advancement comes with more responsibility. And if you want God to raise you up this year, you better get ready for one thing: The Syrians.

Syrians are those people who are so obsessed with you that they put their own life on hold in order to try and bring you down. They want to know where you live, what you do outside of work, they take time to study you, study your weaknesses, they look for a point of entry in which they can attack. Syrians will try to befriend you so that you mistake their interest in you for something positive. But yet they only want what you have.

This type of an enemy is so dangerous because they will not stop at anything until they get your position, until they get your job, until they get your spouse/partner. **But with God, and through prayer, you can begin to shut them down in Jesus name!**

I don't want you to be ignorant; no you must know the truth! If you want to have a position of authority or be married to a person of fame, you must know that "secret admirers" come with the territory. They WILL show up. That is why this year... your relationship with God is so important, your prayers are so important, your adherence to prophetic instruction is so important. For if you are not careful, if you make yourself vulnerable and don't strengthen and pay attention to your weak points, this enemy will become a stronghold in your life.

When you have somebody that is so obsessed with you ... make sure that you don't make their problems to become your problem. When you have somebody that is so obsessed with you ... don't take your focus off of God in order to try and deal with them. When you have somebody that is so obsessed with you ... you must just get into prayer quickly and deal with them. You must know how to deal with this spirit in the right way, for the more you try to fight them in the physical, the harder they will push back.

But I decree and I declare: Anyone that is obsessed with you, that wants to tear you down, every control freak who wants to bring your life to nothing, we command them to die by fire! Whosoever has been monitoring you in order to find your weakness, monitoring you in the working place, spending all their time gathering info that they can use against you, may the Lord blind them in Jesus name!

This year may God give you wisdom to deal with your enemies. May you not fear the Syrians when they show up. May you have such confidence in your heart. Just leave them be. Leave them with their problems. Leave them with their obsession. And know that what God has given you, no man or woman can take it away. Don't fight them. Just pray for God to blind them.

Yes it's time now you need to get into serious prayer: anyone who is obsessed with you, if their motive is wrong, may the Lord blind them. And may God open up the eyes of anyone whose heart is for you.

> When the servant of the man of God got up and went out early the next morning, an army with horses and chariots had surrounded the city. "Oh no, my lord! What shall we do?" the servant asked.
>
> "Don't be afraid," the prophet answered. "Those who are with us are more than those who are with them."
>
> And Elisha prayed, "Open his eyes, Lord, so that he may see." Then the Lord opened the servant's eyes, and he looked and saw the hills full of horses and chariots of fire all around Elisha.

As the enemy came down toward him, Elisha prayed to the Lord, "Strike this army with blindness." So he struck them with blindness, as Elisha had asked. (2 Kings 6:15-18)

12 Prayer Points To Destroy Every Spirit of Frustration & Obsession

(YOU MUST PRAY 13 TIMES TODAY)

1. I take authority over anyone in my father's house, in my mother's house who is obsessed with destroying my life and my family, I rebuke them, I bind them, I command them to die by fire!

2. I take authority over anyone who has been monitoring my movements through spiritual powers in order to capture my destiny, I rebuke you, I bind you, I command you to die by fire!

3. I take authority over anyone who has been monitoring my financial movements through spiritual powers in order to destroy my destiny, I rebuke you, I bind you, I command you to die by fire in the name of Jesus Christ!

4. I take authority over anyone who has been monitoring my relationship/marriage, my .... movements through spiritual powers in order to destroy my destiny, I rebuke you, I bind you, I command you to die by fire in the name of Jesus Christ!

5. I take authority over anyone who has been spying my career, my work, my .... in order to destroy it, I rebuke you, I bind you, I command you to die by fire in the name of Jesus Christ!

6. I take authority over anyone who has been spying my business, my customers, my .... in order to destroy it, I rebuke you, I bind you, I command you to die by fire in the name of Jesus Christ!

7. I take authority over anyone who has been spying my children, my household, my .... in order to destroy it, I rebuke you, I bind you, I command you to die by fire in the name of Jesus Christ!

8. I take authority over any beings such as birds, animals, insects and any other medium that been used to monitor my movements and my progress and report it back to the camp of the enemy, I bind them, I command them to be blind in the name of Jesus Christ.

9. I take authority over anyone or anything that has been assigned to monitor me in order to capture my destiny, I bind them, I command them to be blind in the name of Jesus Christ.

10. This year may the Lord God strike with blindness anything or anyone who is obsessed with destroying my family, my life, my destiny, my .... in the name of Jesus Christ!

11. This year may the Lord God strike with blindness anything or anyone who is obsessed with destroying my health, my mind, my body, my .... through witchcraft, in the name of Jesus Christ!

12. I declare and I decree that this year I am becoming greater and greater in the name of Jesus Christ. This is my year to become a celebrity and be famous in life in Jesus name!

Now angels thou are loosed! Go forth and bring a physical manifestation of these prayers and words that I have spoken in Jesus mighty name.

DAY TWENTY

"The Sidonians"

> There was never anyone like Ahab, who sold himself to do evil in the eyes of the Lord, urged on by Jezebel his wife. (1 Kings 21:25)

I saw in the spirit, throughout the past 3 weeks, you have become a strong and mighty man, a strong and mighty woman. God has begun something great in you, and as you have finished this journey, I declare you will always finish well in anything you do this year. Yes I see the Lord is just beginning to raise you up, in a matter of months you will begin to see the plans and the purposes of Almighty God unveiling for your life.

But, as this favor and promotion meets you this year, there will be another person there to meet you. They will want to seize control of your possession, they will want to seize control of your destiny, they will want to take everything that God has given you and leave you with nothing. Yes, they are called the Sidonians. Remember these are not people that you find while you are in the wilderness or while you are on the way, no they only show up once you have arrived to your destination, once God has brought you in to your promise land.

As we are about to finish, one thing has come out, yes I saw that every time you start something, as soon as you put everything in order, suddenly someone will come into your life and begin to try and take control. Listen, you began the journey and I declare this year you are the only driver who is qualified to drive your life. You are the master of your own destiny.

One of the most wicked people in the Bible, a woman named Jezebel, was a Sidonian.

Sidonians will urge you to make the wrong decisions, they will feed you the wrong advice, they will cause you to shut out every good and favorable person in your life. They are obsessed with control and must always have the upper hand. Listen anyone who wants to forcefully control your life through deceit, I rebuke them and I command them to die by fire. This year, on your journey to success, please don't make stupid decisions like in the past.

Sidonians are so forceful; they must always have their way no matter the cost. This is what destroys marriages, great companies, great athletes, musicians and achievers in life. This is what brings great men and women down. People with great destiny, people who are called and anointed by God, if they are not careful, will be brought down by a Sidonian! That's why as from today you are about to receive special power to overcome them. You are the master of your own destiny.

I prophesy into your life: Anyone who wants to control you in order to mess you up and lead you away from the favor of God, may they die by fire! Yes anyone who wants to manipulate you into making decisions that will bring a curse upon your household, may God deal with them. This year, may you be in charge of your own destiny! This year, may you take back your life. Yes anyone that is trying to forcefully divert you from the plans and purposes of Almighty God in your life, let them be exposed, let them die by fire! Whosoever is planning to cut off your future, to cut off your destiny, we command them to be exposed! Anyone who wants to cut off those around you who are capable of blessing you, die by fire!

This year your eyes must be on constant watch! Just because you are about to finish your 21 Days Fasting & Prayer doesn't mean that you no longer have to pray. No let this only be the beginning. Now that you know what to expect you must begin to put it to work, spiritually and practically.

Begin to do a survey of your life, survey those around you, when you find those people who always want to push their own agenda, urging you to make decisions that you have no peace about, mark those people. Begin to eliminate them, begin to distance yourself. And always stand your ground; learn how to say no. Stop allowing everyone else to rule your life. This year you must take back control of what belongs to you! Don't allow others to make decisions for you where your career is concerned, where your marriage is concerned, where your health is concerned.

12 Prayer Points To Destroy Every Controlling Spirit

(YOU MUST PRAY 15 TIMES TODAY)

1. Today I take authority over every Sidonian spirit that I have inherited from my fathers house and my mothers house that wants to drive my life to the brink of destruction, I rebuke you, I uproot you, I bind you, I command you to die by fire!

2. Right now I take authority over every Sidonian spirit that has been assigned to forcefully take away my career and my job, I rebuke you, I uproot you, I bind you, I command you to die by fire!

3. Today I declare that anyone who wants to come into my life as a friend, as a family member, as a .... in order to erect demonic altars of destruction, I rebuke you, I command you to be exposed and die by fire!

4. Right now I take authority over every strange altar that has been raised up in order to confuse me and take over my life, I rebuke you, I tear you down in the name of Jesus!

5. Right now I take authority over every strange altar that has been raised up in order to control me and take over my life, my destiny, my ...., I rebuke you, I tear you down in the name of Jesus.

6. Right now I take authority over every strange altar that has been raised up in order to steal from me, to steal from my children, to steal from my family, to steal from my .... and take over my life, I rebuke you, I tear you down in the name of Jesus.

7. Right now I take authority over every strange altar that has been raised up in order to abuse me, abuse my ...., and take over my life, I rebuke you, I tear you down in the name of Jesus.

8. Right now I take authority over every strange altar that has been raised up in order to confuse my children, my family, my husband/wife, my .... and take over my life, I rebuke you, I tear you down in the name of Jesus.

9. Every Jezebel spirit that wants to forcefully take control of my financial resources, I bind you, I rebuke you, I command you to die by fire!

10. Every Jezebel spirit that wants to forcefully take control of my business, career, children, my marriage, my relationships, my vision, I bind you, I rebuke you, I command you to die by fire!

11. Right now I take authority over every strange altar that has been raised up in order to control my life through potential health problems, through legal problems, and any other problems, I rebuke you, I tear you down in the name of Jesus.

12. This year I declare and I decree that I am a master of my own destiny; I prophesy that my star is shining brighter and brighter every day in the name of Jesus Christ!

Now angels thou are loosed! Go forth and bring a physical manifestation of these prayers and words that I have spoken in Jesus mighty name.

DAY TWENTY-ONE

"The Philistines"

After the Philistines had captured the ark of God, they took it from Ebenezer to Ashdod. Then they carried the ark into Dagon's temple and set it beside Dagon. When the people of Ashdod rose early the next day, there was Dagon, fallen on his face on the ground before the ark of the Lord! They took Dagon and put him back in his place. But the following morning when they rose, there was Dagon, fallen on his face on the ground before the ark of the Lord! His head and hands had been broken off and were lying on the threshold; only his body remained. (1 Samuel 5:1-4)

I saw a spirit of intimidation, something or someone that always wants to belittle you and make you feel unworthy and unable to do what God has appointed you to do. Yes this spirit always wants to keep sending you back to the drawing board.

This territorial spirit is known as the Philistine spirit; it tried to intimidate Israel through Samson by gouging his eyes out. It tried to intimidate the children of Israel by capturing the Ark of Covenant but for two days God forced their idol god to fall down before the ark, breaking its head and legs. Listen anyone who wants to intimidate you before a crowd, before people, before your family members; we command them to die by fire. This year every demonic setup in order to humiliate you, God will turn it against your enemies. May God humiliate every strange powers that are trying to bring you down.

Right now as you begin to pray you are about to receive power; yes I see supernatural strength for you to be victorious.

The days of your progress and achievement being reversed are over; the days of you being sent back again to the point of wastage and having to start all over again are finished in the name of Jesus Christ. I have the final prayer points for you to declare and decree: No more intimidation in your life and destiny. The game is over for all your enemies.

This year, as you have put God first, there will never be a challenge that rises up that God will not enable you to meet! No Canaanite, No Hivite, No Hittite, No Jebusites, No Amorite, No Girgashite, will keep you from your Promise Land, for the Lord has surely driven them out before you!

12 Prayer Points To Destroy Every Spirit of Intimidation

(YOU MUST PRAY 15 TIMES TODAY)

1. I take authority over every Philistine spirit of intimidation that I have inherited from my father's house and my mother's house, I rebuke you, I bind you, I command you to die by fire in the name of Jesus.

2. Every spirit of intimidation that has been assigned to reverse my achievements this year, I rebuke you, I bind you, I command you to die by fire in the name of Jesus Christ.

3. Every spirit of intimidation that has been assigned to reverse my financial achievements this year, I rebuke you, I bind you, I command you to die by fire in the name of Jesus Christ.

4. Every spirit of intimidation that has been assigned to reverse my daily/monthly/yearly progress, I rebuke you, I bind you, I command you to die by fire in the name of Jesus Christ.

5. Every spirit of intimidation that has been assigned to reverse my relationship/marriage, my children, my achievements, my .... I rebuke you, I bind you, I command you to die by fire.

6. I take authority over every Philistine spirit that has been assigned to intimidate me in public in order to break my confidence, I rebuke you, I bind you, I command you to die by fire in the name of Jesus Christ.

7. Every curse that has been activated over my life through witchcraft in order to reverse my achievements and

progress, I nullify it now and I render it helpless and powerless over my life in the name of Jesus Christ.

8. Every Philistine spirit that is after my spiritual progress and achievements, I rebuke you, I bind you, I command you to die by fire in the name of Jesus Christ.

9. Every Philistine spirit that is after my career, investments, progress and achievements, I rebuke you, I bind you, I command you to die by fire in the name of Jesus Christ.

10. I declare and I decree that this year I am ready for anything and equal to anything through Christ who infuses inner strength into me.

11. I declare and I decree that this year I receive the power and the anointing to go higher and higher in everything that I do in the name of Jesus Christ.

12. I declare and I decree that this year I am becoming greater and greater in the mighty name of Jesus Christ.

TESTIMONIES

We've included some testimonies as a result of the Powerful 21 Days Fasting & Prayer Revival that we held at our London Branch this year. These testimonies are from those who attended live in person or via online our daily Live broadcast. Rejoice and be encouraged by these testimonies and know for sure that what God has done for others, He will do for you.

SHE WAS SUPPOSED TO BE FIRED BUT GOD MADE A WAY

"Man of God I thank you for this 21 Days Revival and I give God all the glory. I work with an agency as a nurse which means we work on contract for a specific time. But my contract for the last two years has been open, it was never assigned an end date. So last year I was told by my managers that at the end of the year all those working with agency would be let go because the Trust Fund is making a lot of cutbacks and doesn't have the money to pay us anymore. On Jan 1 we had the first day of the 21 Day Revival, I was even planning not to stay for the service because I was so pre-occupied with my job situation but I decided to stay and you spoke about fear and we prayed. All this time I was just wrestling with fear about what would happen to my job. But I believe I received the victory. The following day I returned to work, not knowing what will happen. Just then I was told that my manager was looking for me urgently. I called her on my phone and she asked me to wait for her and that she was on her way. When she came she sat down with me and said, 'Something very strange has happened that I need to discuss with you. It's true that all the agency workers were let go because there is no money in the Trust to fund them, but we discovered that your salary has never been funded from the Trust, but from an outside source. We tried to contact the person who is responsible for setting that up in the system, but they seem to have disappeared. So as we cannot confirm anything and from what we see your salary is being funded from outside, you can continue working here, your position is not affected!' Man of God I just want to say thank you for this 21 Days Fasting & Prayer Revival. Amazing things are taking place" – N.M. from London

NO MORE DECEPTION

"Man of God, I live far but I made it up in my mind that I will be here every day for the 21 Day Revival. That means I only get about 2 hours of sleep per night but I counted it worthy. And things have begun to happen. Last year I was deceived into joining a certain business, and it just took over my life. It got to the point where I was coming late for church, I wasn't praying, I even quit my profession to do this business full time. But all I got was stress and headache. I was struggling in every area, I did not even tell you because I felt ashamed. Then yesterday my eyes were opened after you preached about the Hivite spirit, my manager emailed me to say that she refuses for me to quit and I knew that it was God. I have returned to my job and have dumped this business once and for all. Now I have peace again. Thank you for this powerful revelation and Revival." – S.B from Kent, UK

SCAMMERS EXPOSED

"I have always tried to help people out of the goodness of my heart, but after the 3rd day of the fasting I was praying that God would reveal anyone in my life who had been trying to sink my finances. Shortly after, I found out that some of my friends had been using my details and personal information for fraudulent activities! I was in shock, but I thank God for these prayers that exposed them." (S.M from Angola)

ALL PAIN GONE!

"Bishop, at the time I began the fasting I had been having pain in my head every time I wake up in the morning. This had been going on for years. But you told us that we need to chop River Jordan. I began chopping, chopping, chopping. That night I slept like a baby and when I woke up there was no more pain, since that day the pain has not returned. Thank you Jesus!" (Jane K from Lansing, Michigan)

PROPHETIC NUMBERS BRING FAVOR AND MIRACLE MONEY!

"Before we begun the 21 Days Fasting Revival, Bishop said that this year there will be two numbers which represent favor, numbers 3 and 7. Whenever we see those numbers, we can know that favor is around the corner.

Last year I purchased a car and there was a bit of a delay in the car being delivered to me but I have been driving it now for almost a month. But on the 3rd day of the Fasting, I received a check in the mail from the company with an apology letter for the delay and a cheque for £170. Shortly after I received another cheque for £70 and it came from an unknown account whose account number contained two 3's and three 7's. I thank God for this favor as the man of God prophesied and thanks to these prayers and fasting, this year has started well!" (L.M. from UK)

PUT YOUR FAITH TO WORK

"THE SEED"

The testimonies you read above are a result of those who faithfully attended our 21 Day Prayer & Fasting Conference in London (either in person or online) and fully participated in the fasting, the prayers, and the divine instructions which included seed sowing. This part is the missing link between why many have succeeded and others have failed. If you want complete breakthrough, then don't miss this step. I have included for you below the Days 1-21 with their corresponding seeds. Pray about it and ask God to lead you. This is a spiritual journey that you have begun and I pray you would make every effort to shut down your enemies once and for all.

Days 1,2,3&4 – £21 for 21 Days
Day 5 – £26.60 (According to 2 Kings 6:6)
Day 6 – £14 (According to 2x7) or £21 (3x7)
Day 7 – £27 (According to Psalms 27:1-2)
Day 8 – £23 (According to Numbers 23:23)
Day 9 – £20.15 (According to Job 20:15)
Day 10 – £20.15 (According to Job 20:15)
Day 11 – £21.50 (According to Song of Songs 2:15)
Day 12 – £54 (According to Isaiah 54:2)
Day 13 – £21 (According to Numbers 21)
Day 14 – £21.7 (According to 2 Tim 1:7)
Day 15 – £17 (According to Isaiah 54:17)
Day 16 – £27 (According to Psalms 27:2)
Day 17 – £19 (According to Nahum 1:9)
Day 18 – £52 (According to Psalms 52:5)
Day 19 – £13 (According to Psalms 27:13)

118

Day 20 – £28 (According to Deut 28:13)
Day 21 – £41.30 (According to Philippians 4:13)

ABOUT THE MINISTRY

Bishop Climate Ministries is the Healing & Deliverance Ministry founded by Bishop Climate under the anointing and direction of the Holy Spirit. God has anointed Bishop Climate with incredible power to set the captives free. Many people who were unable to get deliverance anywhere else find their freedom as they attend special deliverance sessions conducted through this ministry. The vision of Bishop Climate Ministries is to reach over 1 billion people with the message of deliverance and prosperity, especially in understanding the things of the spirit. Many people are bound because of lack of knowledge and one of the goals of this ministry is to set people free through education.

OTHER BOOKS BY THE AUTHOR

All of our Books are available on Amazon

Deliverance Series Vol. 1-28
New Promises (Power of Confession)
Over The Top
A Conquering Christian
The Law of Wealth – 10 Keys to Financial Freedom
Tithe: The Key to Prosperity
The Truth About Dreams

Order Enquiries: Please visit Amazon, call our offices or order online at www.bishopclimate.me

For Donations/Sowing Seed:

Please visit online www.prophetclimate.net/donate or call our offices at 44 207 738 3668 (UK)
1 347 708 1449 (USA)

You can also send us an email at admin@bishopclimate.org and a member of our team will get back to you shortly.

Simple yet complex
follow simple instruction

- Belong to God
- Do something different
- You have to do something then God will stare a spirit of a destroyer destroying wind + A spirit

Spend time + energy rebuilding

Modern Day AE rebuilding

Stick w:
- PRAY
- PLAN
- REBUILD

Printed in Poland
by Amazon Fulfillment
Poland Sp. z o.o., Wrocław